ELIHU YALE

THE BOOK OF THE
YALE PAGEANT

21 OCTOBER 1916

IN COMMEMORATION OF THE TWO HUN-
DREDTH ANNIVERSARY OF THE REMOVAL
OF YALE COLLEGE TO NEW HAVEN

EDITED BY
GEORGE HENRY NETTLETON

NEW HAVEN, CONNECTICUT
YALE UNIVERSITY PRESS
MDCCCCXVI

FOREWORD

The Book of the Yale Pageant, like the Pageant itself, aims to interpret the significance of Yale in the light of her history and traditions. For Yale is at heart a historic university. Pageant and Book alike unite many voices in utterance of a common loyalty. For Yale is in spirit a community. And Pageant and Book, by together recalling the birthright and inheritance of Yale, seek to suggest a prophecy while they record a history. For the enduring tradition of Yale is service.

The Yale Pageant is essentially an expression of the University rather than of the individual. In the Book which is its permanent memorial it seems inappropriate to emphasize individual services. Its contributors are either directly affiliated with Yale or peculiarly associated with her in service to the community and to the nation. To them and to the various officers, committees, and organizations listed elsewhere in the Book much is due. But only the coöperation with them of many here unnamed has made possible the community Pageant of the City and of the University.

TABLE OF CONTENTS

THE PAGEANT

CONTENTS

MUSIC OF THE YALE PAGEANT

FANFARE ....William Edwin Haesche

PRELUDE ....David Stanley Smith

FIRST OR COLONIAL EPISODE ....Seth Daniels Bingham

FIRST INTERLUDE ....Walter Ruel Cowles

SECOND OR REVOLUTIONARY EPISODE ....Harry Benjamin Jepson

SECOND INTERLUDE ....Horatio William Parker

THIRD OR EARLY NINETEENTH CENTURY EPISODE ..Douglas Stuart Moore

THIRD INTERLUDE ....William Edwin Haesche

FOURTH OR MODERN EPISODE ....David Stanley Smith

FINALE ....David Stanley Smith

ILLUSTRATIONS

The seal of the City of New Haven is reproduced on the cover of *The Book of the Yale Pageant* by permission of the Mayor of the City; the seal of Yale University, by permission of the President and Fellows of Yale University.

The wood-cuts in the book are contributed by Mr. George Henry Langzettel, Secretary of the Yale School of the Fine Arts.

The portraits of Edwards, Cooper, Webster, and Morse are reproduced, by permission, from engravings in *Memorials of Eminent Yale Men,* by Reverend Anson Phelps Stokes; the view of Camp Putnam, 1832, from a copy in possession of Mr. Edwin Oviatt; the signature of Elihu Yale from an original letter in possession of the Elizabethan Club; and many of the remaining views and documents from the collections of the University Library, by permission of Mr. Andrew Keogh, University Librarian.

THE BOOK OF
THE YALE PAGEANT

In glad libation from the brimming Bowl
Pour offering now of pageantry and song;
See where, all iris-hued in robe and stole,
Streams to the sward an Eleusinian throng;
And as one mystic maze unfolds another
Melodious numbers name the mighty mother,
Our harvest-crowned Demeter of the soul.

We that are young look forward and afar
Through dim perspectives of aerial light,
And where the veiling heavens obscurest are
There sits she still, high-throned and benedight,
Her beaconing lustres ever clear and crescent,—
As in December twilights, incandescent
Over the dark verge, glitters love's own star.

We that are old find mellower radiance shed
Down the far vistas of her yester-eves;
Dearer to us the homely days long fled,
The stubbled wheat-fields and the garnered sheaves;
We, loiterers still among the frosted fallows,
Wave welcome to the storied pomp that hallows
The harvest-home of our majestic dead.

Peers of the realms of thought! Your spirit-sway
Is potent yet through our obscurer air;
Men pass, but LIGHT AND TRUTH abide alway,
Like those twin stars that gem the Gorgon's hair,
One flaring through the night, the whole world's wonder,
One dark,—until the veil was torn asunder
As she swung steadfast through her sister's day.

And you, our patriot dead! The azure sky
And the soul's sunlight were your just domain;
But when the nation's evil hour drew nigh
Your genius kindled at her cries of pain,
And flaming through the clouds that overcast her
Lit the deep shadows of her dark disaster
With love that dies not, though the lover die.

Enough. Our praise rings empty and uncouth;
In vain the curling incense-wreaths arise
From the rekindled altars of our youth,
If our hearts bleed not in the sacrifice.
A tinsel pageant this, a puppet-motion,
Save as the cleansing fires of self-devotion
Reconsecrate our lives to LIGHT AND TRUTH.

Dear Mother, doubt not; penetrant and pure
The fire flames inward; we, your children still,
Accept the brand of our investiture,—
Sealed to the service of the living will
Whereby, across the shoreless darkness driven,
Are shepherded the streaming stars of heaven,
While in the soul's abyss love reigns secure.

PRELUDE

THE MEETING OF MARGARET AP IEN-KYN AND ELLIS AP GRIFFITH ON THE BOUNDARIES OF HIS ES-TATE ON THE OCCASION OF THEIR MARRIAGE

By

FREDERICK ERASTUS PIERCE

In 1485, Margaret, daughter of Ienkyn ap Ievan of the Bodidris family, married Ellis ap Griffith of Cwyddelwern Raglot of the Commote of Penllyn, the thirteenth in line from one Dominus Otho, presumedly of the Gherardini family of Florence, who passed over into Normandy and thence to England in 1057, and became so great a favorite of Edward, the Confessor that he excited the jealousy of the Saxon thanes. His son is mentioned in the Doomsday Book as Castellan of Windsor. This son commences the family's connection with Wales by his marriage to Gladys, daughter of Rhiwallon ap Cynfyn, and their son, by taking part in the Norman invasion of that principality and by another Welsh marriage, established the family there. Margaret brought with her as part of her dowry the reversion of the manor of Plas yn Yale, from which her grandson, John Yale, took for the first time the family name.

As the scene opens there enters on one side the procession of Margaret in the following order:

BANNERET   MAN AT ARMS   MAN AT ARMS   BANNERET

MAN AT ARMS   MAN AT ARMS   MAN AT ARMS   MAN AT ARMS

SENESCHAL
EINION AP IORWERTH

SILENTARY   STEWARD
LLEWELYN AP MADOC   RHYS AP OWEN

PAGE   PAGE

PAGE   PAGE

PAGE   PAGE

PAGE   PAGE

MARGARET BODIDRIS AP IENKYN

IENKYN AP IEVAN   TUDOR AP IEVAN
(her father)   *(her uncle)*

BRIDESMAID   BRIDESMAID   BRIDESMAID   BRIDESMAID

BRIDESMAID   BRIDESMAID   BRIDESMAID   BRIDESMAID

EFA AP DYFED
*(her mother, in
a litter)*

PRIEST OF THE HOUSEHOLD

WOMAN OF THE BED CHAMBER   WOMAN OF THE BED CHAMBER
GENWHYFER AP OWEN   MALI AP VYCHAN

WOMAN OF THE BED CHAMBER   WOMAN OF THE BED CHAMBER
NESTA AP OWEN   LOWRIE AP PWYL

RETINUE OF LADIES AND GENTLEMEN

MAN AT ARMS   MAN AT ARMS   MAN AT ARMS   MAN AT ARMS

BANNERET   MAN AT ARMS   MAN AT ARMS   BANNERET

Ellis, with a cavalcade of twelve Companions at Arms, rides in from the other side, followed by a religious procession and School of Bards. The two processions meet; and Ellis and his companions dismount and uncover while the bride and bridegroom are blest by the Priest. Ellis kneels to kiss Margaret's hand.

Ellis. The happiest day that ever dawned on Wales
     Is that which brings thee, Margaret. See, thy husband
     Comes no harsh master but thy kneeling slave.
Margaret. Master for life, dear husband. Mount and ride.
Ellis. Shall I obey my tongue-tied queen or pause?
     What dawning thoughts have called the rosy clouds
     Across that lovely cheek, one moment back
     As white as wintry Snowdon?
Margaret.   Spare me, Ellis.
     If I am queen then mount and ride with me.
Ellis. To church or home or death at Margaret's word.

  (They re-mount, and the whole procession rides off in pairs, Ellis
       and Margaret leading.)

Ellis. Why silent, Mistress bride? That merry tongue,
     That twittered night and day like birds in trees,
     Has it no word of all its wealth for me?
     You seem like one who gazed with second sight.
Margaret. Perhaps I do, dear Ellis. Is it vision,
     Or the wild dream of a much moved girl bride?
     The low, encircling hills round this green valley,
     What cover them, my husband?
Ellis.   Shrubs and trees.
Margaret. So I believed, but now they seem alive
     With hazy forms, that, many thousand strong,
     Gaze down on us. They look not of our age,
     And yet our bridal seems to make them glad.
     Are they ghosts or are we? Their eyes are kind,
     And a low murmuring ripple of applause
     Blows down the wind to greet us. Ellis, hark!
     Something they said of children born of us.
Ellis. Nothing is there but trees that wave in wind.
     Your hand, sweet bride. This dream, if dream it were,
     Was a good omen. Hush, the bards begin.

SONG OF THE WELSH BARDS

Low, lulling notes and sweet
Fit well the hour we sing;
Notes grand and solemn greet
The years that hour may bring.
Come, bards of Cambria, come, soul keyed and hand on string.

As light and storm-cloud blent
Build up the rainbow span,
Lovelier than light's blue tent,
Or storm's embattled van,
So life's full glory first crowns wedded maid and man.

Round rapture's Iris bow
Far futures lean and peer,
Glad lives earth yet may know,
Great hopes that ever near.
Bridegrooms hear worlds to be in that sweet voice they hear.

What race derived from thee
Shall those far aeons show?
Great conquerors yet to be,
But not with blade and bow.
They spread the realm of thought, crowned kings that will and know.

Wake, peaks where snows are piled;
Ring, every Cambrian vale.
Pure manhood, firm and mild,
Ye bore; it shall not fail,
Nor wither from the world while loving lips name Yale.

Hers the deep organ's peal,
And lightning's guided gleam;
The saviour hands that heal;
The bard's and scholar's dream;
The painter's art; the laws that chasten and redeem;

Calm faith when nations doubt;
Green woods where hills were bare.
Caermarthen's echo, shout;
Plinlimmon, laugh in air.
Ye winds of Wales, blow glad to greet our bridal pair.

And hers the solemn code,
As grand as Arthur's own,
That man in God's abode
Lives not for self alone.
Great Snowdon, thrill to hear, and Idris' chair of stone.

Brave groom, love well thy bride.
The truth our lips aver.
Oblivion's veil may hide
Ten thousand brides that were;
Four centuries hence and more great men shall honor her.

(The processions move off together followed by the bards.)

BANNERET   MAN AT ARMS   MAN AT ARMS   BANNERET

MAN AT ARMS   MAN AT ARMS   MAN AT ARMS   MAN AT ARMS

SENESCHAL
EINION AP IORWERTH

SILENTARY   STEWARD
LLEWELYN AP MADOC   RHYS AP OWEN

PAGE   PAGE

PAGE   PAGE

PAGE   PAGE

PAGE   PAGE

MARGARET BODIDRIS AP IENKYN

IENKYN AP IEVAN   TUDOR AP IEVAN
(her father)   *(her uncle)*

BRIDESMAID   BRIDESMAID   BRIDESMAID   BRIDESMAID

BRIDESMAID   BRIDESMAID   BRIDESMAID   BRIDESMAID

EFA AP DYFED
(her mother, in
a litter)

PRIEST OF THE HOUSEHOLD

WOMAN OF THE BED CHAMBER   WOMAN OF THE BED CHAMBER
GENWHYFER AP OWEN   MALI AP VYCHAN

WOMAN OF THE BED CHAMBER   WOMAN OF THE BED CHAMBER
NESTA AP OWEN   LOWRIE AP PWYL

RETINUE OF LADIES AND GENTLEMEN

MAN AT ARMS   MAN AT ARMS   MAN AT ARMS   MAN AT ARMS

BANNERET   MAN AT ARMS   MAN AT ARMS   BANNERET

Ellis, with a cavalcade of twelve Companions at Arms, rides in from the other side, followed by a religious procession and School of Bards. The two processions meet; and Ellis and his companions dismount and uncover while the bride and bridegroom are blest by the Priest. Ellis kneels to kiss Margaret's hand.

Ellis.   The happiest day that ever dawned on Wales
             Is that which brings thee, Margaret. See, thy husband
             Comes no harsh master but thy kneeling slave.

Margaret. Master for life, dear husband. Mount and ride.

Ellis.   Shall I obey my tongue-tied queen or pause?
             What dawning thoughts have called the rosy clouds
             Across that lovely cheek, one moment back
             As white as wintry Snowdon?

Margaret.   Spare me, Ellis.
             If I am queen then mount and ride with me.

Ellis.   To church or home or death at Margaret's word.

(*They re-mount, and the whole procession rides off in pairs, Ellis
and Margaret leading.*)

Ellis.   Why silent, Mistress bride? That merry tongue,
             That twittered night and day like birds in trees, .
             Has it no word of all its wealth for me?
             You seem like one who gazed with second sight.

Margaret. Perhaps I do, dear Ellis. Is it vision,
             Or the wild dream of a much moved girl bride?
             The low, encircling hills round this green valley,
             What cover them, my husband?

Ellis.   Shrubs and trees.

Margaret. So I believed, but now they seem alive
             With hazy forms, that, many thousand strong,
             Gaze down on us. They look not of our age,
             And yet our bridal seems to make them glad.
             Are they ghosts or are we? Their eyes are kind,
             And a low murmuring ripple of applause
             Blows down the wind to greet us. Ellis, hark!
             Something they said of children born of us.

Ellis.   Nothing is there but trees that wave in wind.
             Your hand, sweet bride. This dream, if dream it were,
             Was a good omen. Hush, the bards begin.

FIRST OR COLONIAL EPISODE

SCENE I

THE FOUNDING OF NEW HAVEN

By

LEE WILSON DODD

On or about April 15th, 1638, Governor Eaton and his party of colonists arrived at a beautiful harbor in the rocky Connecticut shore, now known as New Haven harbor, but then known as Quinnipiack harbor—"Quinnipiack" being the name of a small tribe of Connecticut Indians inhabiting that region. The Eaton colonists soon discovered this tribe to be in miserable estate. A plague of some sort had ravaged them. But forty-six fighting men remained, and the entire tribe, including squaws and papooses, numbered not more than one hundred and fifty persons. Moreover, this little and sickly band was oppressed by the powerful Mohawk tribe, dwelling to the west of them, and by the fierce Pequots, dwelling to the east. The Quinnipiacks seem, therefore, to have welcomed the English colonizers. Their Sachem, Momauguin, his chiefs, and his sister, Shaumpishuh, willingly made over all their land to Theophilus Eaton and his men, in exchange for protection, and for some dozens of knives, hatchets, English coats, and the like. A reservation, also, was set apart for the tribe.

The Bowl is supposed to represent the Powwow-Place of the Quinnipiacks, on the Fresh Meadows, eastward of the Solitary Cove—now Morris Cove.

Hither the Quinnipiacks come, in solemn procession, bearing with them Shaumpishuh, sister of the Sachem Momauguin, who lies on an improvised stretcher of hemlock boughs, stricken with the evil sickness, and seemingly at point of death.

As the sad little procession advances, the Indian women send up a wailing, a lament, to Gitche Manitou, the Great Spirit.

LAMENT OF THE INDIAN WOMEN

Father of wind,
You have blown, you have blown upon us—
Cold from the East, cold from the North
You have blown upon us!
Father of water, now the waters have started
Running back to the sea;
Father of leaves, the little leaves have started!
Father of grass, the river meadows are green again—
The river meadows are green!
Way-ha-way! You have blown, you have blown upon us,
Cold from the East, cold from the North!
Father of wind, you have blown upon Shaumpishu,
You have blown upon Shaumpishu!
Way-ha-way! and the little leaves have started,
The river meadows are green. . . .
But over them flickers a yellow leaf far-flying,
Torn from us! Way-ha-way!

(*The hemlock-litter, bearing Shaumpishuh, is set down in the center of the Powwow-Place. The Sachem Momauguin and his chiefs stand in a half-circle about it. The Squaws, with their children, and the maidens, draw sadly apart.*)

Momauguin. Let the tepees be pitched, yonder, by the rim of the Great Forest. Let boughs be brought and birch-logs, and a white flame kindled among them. Let the white flame o'erleap the rim of the Great Forest. And let deer be killed, and a feast made. For Shaumpishuh, my sister, lies sorely stricken.

The Tribe (in general outcry).
Way-ha-way! You have blown, you have blown upon us,
Father of wind. . . . .

(*To one side of the Powwow-Place, the Squaws and maidens
pitch the tepees of the tribe. Meanwhile, some of the younger
men bring boughs and birch-logs and kindle a great fire. Others,
with bows and arrows, slip off into the Great Forest. And now
the Medicine Men of the tribe come forward to the litter of
Shaumpishuh. They are clad in bearskins, and their faces are
hideously painted. They have drums and rattles and they circle
about Shaumpishuh, howling and gesticulating, in the Medicine
Dance of their tribe.
Suddenly a Young Warrior of the tribe comes running out
from the edge of the Great Forest. The Medicine Dance breaks
off. The Chiefs gather about him.*)

Young Warrior. Momauguin—they come—they are at hand!
The tribute-takers!
Momauguin. From the place of the Sun's rising, or from
beyond the Shining River?
Young Warrior. From beyond the Shining River.
Momauguin. The tribute-takers of the Mohawks are upon
us. . .
The Chiefs. The tribute-takers of the Mohawks are upon
us. . .
General Outcry. Way-ha-way!

(*A band of warriors of the Mohawk tribe, in full war-paint,
now appears at the rim of the Great Forest. The Sachem
Momauguin makes the peace-sign, and they advance.*)

Momauguin. Warriors from beyond the Shining River, ye
come in an evil hour! Out of a purple cloud a great sickness
has fallen upon us. My braves waste from me like snow from
the meadows when the waters are loosened. (*With a solemn
gesture.*) Lo, Shaumpishuh, the Wise, our Sister! Her eyes
are darkened. . .

The Squaws (*shrilly*). Way-ha-way! You have blown upon Shaumpishuh, Father of wind. . . . .

Leader of the Mohawks. Tribute, O Momauguin, tribute! We come not for lamentations.

Momauguin. Let us sit together, first, and let the Peace Pipe be lighted. Let it pass from hand to hand. . .

(*Momauguin and his chiefs, and the Mohawk braves, seat themselves in a circle about the fire. The Peace Pipe is lighted and passes from hand to hand.*

At a signal from Momauguin, Indian boys race and wrestle, performing feats of skill, and ending with a tribal dance.)

Leader of the Mohawks (*rising*). Tribute, O Momauguin!

Momauguin (*rising*). I am powerless before you. It shall be brought. . .

(*A distant gun-shot is heard. Consternation among the Indians. The Mohawk braves leap to their weapons and draw apart with menacing gestures. A young Quinnipiack brave enters, running at full speed.*)

Young Brave. Pale faces! Pale faces—O Momauguin!

Leader of the Mohawks. Many or few—?

Young Brave. Few—but with thunder-sticks, breathing flame! Who shall stand against them?

Leader of the Mohawks. Tribute, O Momauguin—tribute! That we may depart. . .

Shaumpishuh (*half-rising from her litter*). No tribute—no tribute!

General Outcry. Shaumpishuh! Shaumpishuh speaks!

Shaumpishuh (*more wildly*). Pale faces—pale faces! Bid them welcome, O Momauguin! Bid them welcome! No tribute! No tribute—!

(*She sinks back on her litter.*)

Momauguin (*to the Mohawks*). Shaumpishuh, the Wise, has spoken! No tribute! Get ye gone! . . .

(The Quinnipiack braves catch up their weapons and advance upon the Mohawk warriors, who loose their arrows toward the Quinnipiacks, then, out-numbered, turn and fly. . . Even as they vanish, the sound of men's voices, chanting a Puritan hymn, is heard—at first distantly, then nearer and nearer.)

Momauguin. Pale faces! . . . Shaumpishuh, the Wise, has spoken. . . I go to greet them, and bid them welcome!

(The Quinnipiack braves lay down their weapons, and follow Momauguin, who advances, slowly, majestically, toward the rim of the Forest.

Enter, to them, Theophilus Eaton, Reverend John Davenport, *and other Pilgrims. Four of the band are carrying a great chest. Momauguin and his braves, in dumb show, bid them welcome and lead them to the fire, where the Peace Pipe is again lighted and passed from hand to hand. Fright of the squaws, children, and maidens, at sight of the pale faces. After a time, urged by curiosity, they draw gradually nearer.)*

Theophilus Eaton (to Reverend John Davenport). Mark how they press about us, brother! *(To a younger Pilgrim.)* Thomas Stanton, thou hast skill in the Pequot tongue. Dost thou catch the drift of *this* babble? They seem a gentle and inoffensive tribe.

Thomas Stanton. Ay, they mean us no harm.

Reverend John Davenport. The Lord God of Israel, who hath delivered us from the hands of the Egyptians, wills not that we should perish in the wilderness.

Theophilus Eaton. Nay, brother—for methinks this is indeed a Land of Promise, with wide and well-watered meadows, though something menaced by churlish and secret hills.

Reverend John Davenport (rising). God of our Fathers, God of the Righteous, thou hast steered us over dreary seas to a far country!

(The Colonists rise and stand with bowed heads. The Indian Chiefs rise also and stand motionless.)

May it be Thy will that here, in this savage land, Thy children may find freedom and holy peace. Turn thou the hearts of this naked and trivial race to a knowledge of Thy truth and law. May all things stand accomplished in Thy sight. And Thine be the glory and the power ever and for ever! Amen!

Colonists. Amen. . .

Theophilus Eaton (to certain Colonists). Open now the chest and distribute beads and baubles, such as these children love! For here, and in no spot less favored, shall we make our habitation. (*Seeing Shaumpishuh.*)—Why, what poor creature is this?

Thomas Stanton (after conferring with the Chiefs). Shaumpishuh, sister of the Sachem Momauguin, lies at the point of death.

Reverend John Davenport (kneeling beside her). Nay, she is dead.

(*The Indian women, wailing, gather about Shaumpishuh. Thomas Stanton, at a sign from Theophilus Eaton, confers with Momauguin.*)

Thomas Stanton (to the Colonists). They go to bear the body of Shaumpishuh to the summit of the Great Rock yonder—that some tribal prophecy may be accomplished. There will they make a feast, and yield themselves and their fortunes henceforth wholly to our guidance.

Reverend John Davenport. God's hand is seen in this!

(*The Indians take up the body of Shaumpishuh upon its litter of hemlock-boughs.*)

The Tribe (in general outcry, as before).
Way-ha-way! You have blown, you have blown upon us, Father of wind. . .

(*They bear off the body of Shaumpishuh toward the Great Forest.*)

Theophilus Eaton. Take up the chest, and follow—for though the hand of God guide us, the hearts of these savage folks are fickle—and gifts are gifts!

Reverend John Davenport. Yea, brothers, for God in his wisdom forbids us not to use our wits! Forward then! But let the wild chanting of the ungodly yield now to a nobler Psalm!

Theophilus Eaton. Ay. Well said. Strike up, Thomas Stanton—a Hymn of Thankfulness and Praise. . . It will lighten the way.

(Thomas Stanton sings lustily the first two lines of a Puritan hymn. The Colonists join in the song, and led by Theophilus Eaton and the Reverend John Davenport follow the Quinnipiacks into the Great Forest. As they pass from view the hymn is taken up by invisible choirs and swells to mighty proportions . . . . . .)

Omnibus & Singulis, Has præsentes lecturis
Salutem in Dno. Nobis Notum sit, quod Iohanne
Hart Candidatum, Primum in Artibus gradum
competentem, tam probavimus, quam approbavimus: quem
Examine sufficiente prævio approbatum, Nobis placet
Titulo Graduꝗ Artium Liberalium Baccalaurei adornare
& condecorare. Cuꝗ hoc Instrumentum in membrana
scriptum Testimonium sit. A Gymnasio Academico ⸺
Connecticutensi 17 Calend. Octobr: 1703

Moses Noyrs
Thomas Buckingham
Abadiah Pierson

THE FIRST B.A. YALE DIPLOMA
(John Hart, B.A. Yale, 1703)

SCENE II

THE FOUNDING OF THE COLLEGE

By

EDWARD MORTIMER CHAPMAN

Time, September, 1701. Place, the house of the Reverend Samuel Russell, in Branford. Enter the Reverend Messrs. James Pierpont of New Haven, Abraham Pierson of Killingworth, James Noyes of Stonington, Israel Chauncey of Stratford, Thomas Buckingham of Saybrook, Samuel Andrews of Milford, Timothy Woodbridge of Hartford, Noadiah Russell of Middletown, Joseph Webb of Fairfield, Samuel Russell of Branford. Six of these carry parcels of books.

Russell (of Branford). Reverend Fathers and Brethren, you are welcome to this house, which is honoured by your presence and errand. Though as well-nigh the youngest of your company, it be scarce fitting that I should suggest the ordering of our business, yet I am bold to move that Mr. Pierpont, whose forwardness in these matters of the morning is known to all, do moderate this meeting.

(This motion, seconded, prevails and Pierpont takes the chair.)

Noyes. And further, Sir, since it is the hope of some of us that this business may be remembered unto later days, I move that Mr. Pierson do act as our Scribe and Secretary.

(This motion prevailing and Pierson coming forward, all stand reverently while Pierpont lifts his hands in prayer. They seat themselves.)

Pierpont.   It is scarce needful, Brethren, that I state the object of our conference.   You know right well how early the desire for a College or Collegiate School arose in this Colony.   Nor has it ever slept for very long.   Of late it has bestirred itself with new vigor.   New England has now near to an hundred thousand English.   There are well-nigh forty churches in Connecticut.   For due instruction of the people in the things of God, for the maintenance of a learned and orthodox ministry, and for the right service of the Civil State, we are greatly beholden to take thought.   As we have met upon our various occasions this past summer, our hearts have burned within us, feeling that the acceptable time for action was drawing nigh.   Hence this summons and our present meeting.

Russell (of Middletown).   Has any inquiry been made as to the good-will of Harvard in the matter?   Many of us are her sons.   We owe her much, and have given our best years to her as hostages.   It would ill beseem us lightly to undertake a rival college.

Pierpont.   A fair question and soon answered.   Be it known that among those who have given aid and comfort to our hope are Mr. Secretary Addington and the Honourable Judge Sewall, with weighty suggestions concerning a charter; while those pillars of fire and cloud, the Mathers, have promised help.   They see eye to eye with us, that many towardly youths in this Colony are like to miss their chance and our churches their service because the distance to the Bay is great and the expense heavy. Surely such men speak for Harvard.

Woodbridge.   It is well answered as to Mother Harvard.   But how of Mother England?   Already she thinks us in Connecticut to be somewhat greedy of privilege.   The General Court may approve our purpose to grant degrees, but through what eyes will London see it?

Pierson.   With the Reverend Moderator's permission I would answer that this, too, has been foreseen.   Here is delicate ground upon which it behooves us to go softly; and should we petition

the General Court for a charter, it will be wise to give the right
to grant degrees but an inconspicuous place in our prayer. Better
to call our College a Collegiate School at present. The less shall
thus be made to contain the greater, and he that humbleth himself
be finally exalted.

Noyes. I am an old man, Brethren, and you know how long
this vision has been before mine eyes. The time is come to act.
Our people are awake. The General Court will be favourable.
The men of the Bay will never be more inclined to the enterprise
than at present. And as to Harvard, I look forward to see these
two schools of godly learning become fellow servants, not only
of this New England of ours, but of the other colonies as
well,—ὑπηρέτας, under-rowers-in-the-ship, as the Apostle saith;
their main rivalry being as to which shall row the better.

Buckingham. My neighbour of Stonington speaks soberness
and truth, as is his wont; and right heartily I second him. Let
us act, not only in the direction of a charter, but in that of a local
habitation. I have long known that some of you incline toward
Saybrook. I pray you to confirm yourselves in that opinion.
Though neither numerous nor wealthy, we of Saybrook stand
ready to make sacrifice for the Collegiate School. Indeed, I
believe that already it hath been put into the heart of one man to
provide house and home therefor. Unless I misread the work-
ings of Nathaniel Lynde's mind, he will do it. Some of you
know how the land lies with us. Here (*Drawing with his staff
upon the sanded floor*) is the fort; here the Great River sweeping
to the sea and carrying more West India commerce every year;
here Lady Fenwick's tomb; here, Meeting House and Parsonage;
and here the field where I fondly hope to see the School grow to
a College.

Chauncey. It is a fair dream, my Brother Buckingham; but
whence shall endowments, revenues and books be supplied?

Buckingham. Never fear but that if we do our duty, those
shall be raised up from whom endowment and revenue shall come.
We shall ourselves make a beginning with the books. Then

would I look at home and abroad.   Let the Agent of the Colony in London bestir himself.   Let him even ask men like Sir Edmund Andros.

All (*in amazement*).   Andros!

Buckingham (*stoutly*).   Ay, Andros! For you know, Brethren, that when he was not on the tyrant's errands, there were bowels of mercies in the man.   Yes, and a pretty wit, too. Well I remember the July morning six and twenty years ago when he made his attempt on Saybrook Fort.   It was a time of anxiety.   Our men had marched against the Narragansetts, as Andros doubtless knew.   Never before had my white mare travelled the dusty road to Oyster River so quick.   There Captain Chapman was at home, too old for the wars.   We consulted and sent messengers hot-foot to Hartford.   Leaving the hay-harvest to the women, we gathered what men we might; threw them into the Fort; hoisted the King's standard and shut the gates in Andros' face.   He could not fire upon the standard, or force the gates without firing.   So he must needs chafe and fume, while Providence and the Governor were sending us Captain Bull with all speed; nor was Bull wanting in firmness when he came.   It was a sore disappointment to the enemy; yet Andros must needs have his quip.   "This Bull," quoth he, "should have his horns tipped with silver."   It would suit exactly with his genius to help our School within musket-shot of where he was thus thwarted. Yes, I should ask Andros.

Pierpont.   Bear with me, Brethren, if I interrupt this talk of ways and means, weighty as it is, to say that your resolute faces quite as much as your words have convinced me that the time has come when we can commit ourselves to this adventure in confidence.   Let the General Court and our People know that a beginning has been made and they will not fail us.   So without further parley let us act.   (*Slowly lifts a group of quartos and advances to the table.*)   In solemn hope that by God's Providence great issues may spring from this deed, I give these Books for the founding of a College in this Colony.

Noyes. It is bravely spoken, my friend; nor shall thy hope prove vain. From the easternmost border I come to second thee. I give these Books for the founding of a College in this Colony.

(*The four others who have brought books present them with the same words.*)

Webb. Brethren, some of us came hither unwarned of the deeper purpose of this meeting or doubtful of its issue. But you shall not find us wanting in zeal or sacrifice. We are committed with you. Such volumes as our own scanty stores can furnish and our solicitation gain from friends, shall buttress yours. We have consulted and thus agreed. Count us as having part and lot with you in the founding of a College in this Colony.

Pierpont. So we stand together in a day's work that shall be long remembered. Now as we part, it is fitting that our elder Brother Noyes should invoke the blessing of God to the end that He, who, as we trust, hath thus planted, shall ever nourish and sustain.

(*Noyes lifts his hands in benediction; then all file reverently out.*)

HISTORICAL NOTE

This Episode necessarily moves in the realm of tradition. We cannot say who were present at this Branford meeting; nor, indeed, have we absolute assurance that the meeting took place at all, despite President Clap's embodiment of the story in his rather uncritical narrative of the early days of the College. The tradition, however, seems trustworthy upon the whole. There had probably been various informal conferences of the clergy during the summer of 1701 and there would naturally have been some formal meeting to provide for the petition to the General Court. The Episode supposes that all of the ten original Trustees of the Collegiate School were present with the exception of Samuel Mather of Windsor whose infirm health must have forbidden his attendance.   Samuel Russell of Branford, at whose house the meeting is said to have been held and who was chosen Trustee at the November meeting in Saybrook, is naturally also in attendance.   The dialogue generally follows historical lines.   Secretary Addington and Judge Sewall made important suggestions as to the Charter; Cotton Mather's later letter to Elihu Yale in behalf of the College is of notable interest; and it is possible that the petitioners for a charter made their purpose to grant degrees rather inconspicuous in order to avoid question with the authorities in England.   Andros—who, though regarded as a man of Belial by the colonists, had a generous and hearty side to him— actually gave sundry books some years later.   It seems scarcely probable that all the ministers gave books at this time; there is reason to believe, rather, that some pledged themselves to give later or to solicit gifts from others.

HOUSE OF REVEREND SAMUEL RUSSELL AT BRANFORD
(1701)

SCENE III

THE REMOVAL OF THE BOOKS
FROM SAYBROOK

By

JACK RANDALL CRAWFORD

The scene is Saybrook and the surrounding country in the latter half of the year 1718. Two years before, the little struggling Collegiate School had been removed from Saybrook to New Haven, because the latter had such advantages as the "conveniency of its situation, agreeableness of the air and soil, and probability of providing what will be necessary for the convenience of the scholars as cheap or cheaper than any other places, together with many other weighty considerations." Needless to remark, however, these "weighty considerations" do not seem to have appealed with the same force to the people of Saybrook as they did to the trustees sitting at New Haven. The situation that resulted from this difference of opinion concerning the proper location for the Collegiate School was an early manifestation of that intense civic pride characteristic of many present-day American communities.

Saybrook still possessed the library; let New Haven boast, if it pleased, a few sober young gentlemen in caps and gowns. Scholars could not be made without books any more than bricks without straw. Dr. Daniel Buckingham kept securely locked in the library of his home at Saybrook more than a thousand volumes of choice Latin and orthodox theology. Imagine the plight of the tutors at New Haven, deprived of books and forced to rely for their teaching upon their own knowledge! For a professor such a predicament was not to be endured. Without footnotes, appendices, chapter and verse—how make his words convincing to the youthful mind? Further, how could the youthful mind be furnished with material for study outside of the class-room? It is not surprising, therefore, that the trustees at New Haven were ready to go to any lengths to secure possession of these books.

The first step was a diplomatic one. The trustees prepared and duly forwarded to Dr. Daniel Buckingham the following note: "to deliver to the Rector or his order the books and papers belonging to that College which were left in his house when the said College was moved to New Haven." Dr. Buckingham's reply, while couched in legal form, was unsatisfactory. Politely, but with subtle irony, he sent word back that "he did not know that he had any books belonging to Yale College"—seeming, as one historian pathetically puts it, to deny the new name, for it had always been called the Collegiate School while at Saybrook— "but when he did and should receive authentick orders he would deliver them."

Upon receipt of this communication, the Sheriff received from the trustees the necessary "authentick orders." And at this point, Gentle Reader, if you will turn your eyes downward toward the interior of the Bowl, you will see what happened next.

It is now early December of the year 1718 and the Sheriff is accompanied by his assistants and, let it be supposed, by a few students from New Haven who, having an inkling that stirring actions are afoot, have stolen away contrary both to collegiate authority and to historical fact, in order to take part in this episode. You see the little group on its way toward Saybrook. It is too early for snow, but there is a chill East wind blowing off the Sound which causes the Sheriff to muffle his cloak about him. He is a large gloomy man of pessimistic anticipations. The East wind has intensified his worst suspicions. The students, having escaped for a time from the shackles of the class-room, behave after the manner of their kind upon these occasions. But one college rule they must still adhere to—all their converse and

PRÆCELLENTI ET CELEBERRIMO
VIRO,

D. D. Gurdono Saltonstallo, Armigero,

In Omnifaria Virtute, Scientia, et Literatura, Versatissimo, Coloniæ Connecticutensis GUBERNATORI Inclytissimo, Terque Quaterque Honorando:

ASPECTABILI Etiam Beneficentia, et Generositate Perlucenti

D. D. ELIHU YALE, Londinensi, Armigero,

Suum & Nostrum COLLEGIUM YALENSE, Maximis Muneribus Ornanti ;

VIRO nec non Undiquaque Laudando, summa Pietate, & Prudentia Florenti

D. NATHAN GOLD, Armigero, Coloniæ Præfato, Vice–Gubernatori Meritissimo ;

Deinde hujus Politiæ Connecticutensis SENATORIBUS Maxime Venerandis, Justitiæque Patronis Acerrimis, Ter Honoratis;

Atque simul Reverendissimis, ACADEMIÆ nostræ Procuratoribus, omni Liberali Eruditione, Prudentia, & Sagacitate Decoratis :

Reverendo Pariter, ac pro Doctrinâ, Meritifque, COLLEGII YALENSIS Rectori D. TIMOTHEO CUTLER, (cujus sub Auspiciis ha
Doctrinæ Primitiæ sunt defendendæ) Antititibus etiam Religionis Orthodoxæ, Sanctis, Doctis, Plurimoque Honore, et Reverentia Prosequendis :

Postremo Universis (Ubique Gentium) de Virtute Humanitate, Doctrina, Doctisque bene Merentibus ;

Thesis sequentes, quas (Indulgente Divina Providentia) in Collegio Yalensi, Nos Juvenes in Artibus Neophyti, pro Tenuitate nostra, suomo Molimine defendendas aggredimur :

Ebenezer Wakeman   Daniel Edwards   Ezechias Kilborn
Thomas White   Jonathan Edwards   Abrahamus Nott
Gulielmus Billings   Daniel Kirtland   Johannes Walton
                     Samuel Mix

Damus D. D. Q.

HEADING OF THESIS LIST OF CLASS OF 1720

(Jonathan Edwards, B.A. Yale, 1720)

even their frivolity must be in the Latin tongue. This is a further source of annoyance to the Sheriff who neither understands the learned language, nor properly values this excellent rule.

The little group of men is now in the near vicinity of Saybrook.

Sheriff's Assistant. We are on the edge of Saybrook township. Have you your warrant secure, Caleb?

Sheriff. Aye—here it is. (*Draws forth a paper which the wind flutters. Several gather about him to read.*)

Sheriff (*adjusting his horn spectacles*). My instructions are "to demand the said books and upon his refusal to enter into the house." I shall do my duty in the sight of the Lord.

1st Student (*ironically*). Fidem publicam servavit Cicero.

Sheriff (*to the 1st Student*). I know nothing of that, but it is written, "it is as sport to a fool to do mischief: but a man of understanding hath wisdom."

(*The other Students laugh.*)

2nd Student (*laughing*). Virum omnigenae doctrinae non levi tinctura imbutum!

1st Student (*annoyed that the Sheriff has turned the joke on him*). Facile ridet stultus! Qui cupit exemplum, captet hic egregium.

Sheriff (*looking toward an approaching group of Saybrook people*). Cease your heathenish gibberish—here's soon work to do.

2nd Student (*indicating the Sheriff*). Quid consilii Caesaris est? Cives Sabrookienses appropinquant.

(*Several farmers are seen busy about their tasks. Some are loading ox-carts, others ploughing. Another group of townsmen is seen discussing the Sheriff and his group. Dr. Daniel Buckingham detaches himself from his fellow townsmen and advances to meet the Sheriff.*)

Buckingham (*with dignity*). I greet ye, strangers, in the name of the Lord.

Sheriff. Dr. Buckingham, greetings. We are come from New Haven.

Buckingham. What is your mission to Saybrook?

Sheriff (*produces his warrant*). I have here a warrant, drawn by due process of law, bidding me demand, in the name of the trustees of Yale College, the books held by you. Furthermore I am empowered to enter your house and take possession of the said books.

(*The Saybrook citizens gather about with murmurs and threats.*)

Buckingham. I have no books belonging to Yale College— but I have the library of the Collegiate School of Saybrook. Therefore, Sheriff, if you enter my house, it shall be upon your peril. I shall defend my trust with all the means in my power!

(*The Saybrook citizens shout approval.*)

1st Student (*aside to 2nd Student*). Libros haberet magno sui cum periculo.

2nd Student (*replying to 1st Student*). Peritus rerum belli non est. Quid sibi vult?

Sheriff. You must not threaten me, Dr. Buckingham, I shall do my duty! Resistance to the law—.

Buckingham. Resistance to fiddlesticks, sir! I know my rights! The books shall stay in Saybrook.

(*He starts to walk away. The Saybrook citizens gather angrily about him with shouts:* "We will stand with you, Doctor Daniel!" "He shan't have the books!" *etc.*)

Sheriff (*to his men*). Requisition those ox-carts in the name of the law!

(*The Students shout with delight. The Sheriff's assistants go toward the farmers and their carts.*)

Students (*shouting*). Proelium committit! Maturandum est nobis!

(They help to drive the farmers away from the ox-carts and lead the wagons toward Dr. Buckingham's house. Some of the Saybrook citizens aim stones at the Students, who reply with even greater zest.)

1st Saybrook Citizen (taking the leadership). I have a plan to beat these New Haven thieves! Break down the Bridge!

Saybrook Citizens (some running toward the bridge). The Bridge! Aye—the Bridge! Break it down. Obadiah, where is thy ax?

2nd Saybrook Citizen (rushing toward the bridge). Here it is, by the blessing of Providence!

(Obadiah, who is a lusty youth in homespun, swings great smashing blows at the bridge over a brook on the road to New Haven. Several other Saybrook citizens join him, while others renew their attacks upon the ox-carts.)

1st Student (as a citizen tries to pull him off the ox-cart). Non satis praesidii—for—for—by Virgil's Aeneid, Ezekiel, what is the Latin for ox-cart?

2nd Student (rushing to his assistance). Bos, bovis—I know not—non hostibus parcitur! *(He has a violent encounter with a 3rd Saybrook citizen.)* Vim facio—I'll show thee, thou lantern jawed oysterman—poenas repeto—thou dweller on a dank marsh—praesto Gallis virtute—I'll send thee secundo flumine—there! *(As Saybrook citizen falls.)*—se sustinere non potest! Veni-vidi-vici!

3rd Saybrook Citizen. Help! Help! This young ruffian from New Haven is casting a spell upon me—he has invoked a legion of devils and I am spent! He calls upon evil spirits by their names! *(To the Student.)* Thou shalt lie in the stocks for this, or my name is not Ebenezer Doolittle.

2nd Student (dashing after the ox-cart). Magnae fuit fortunae—for thee that I didn't break thy head, Ebenezer!

(All over the stage similar encounters are going on, while the Sheriff's men finally succeed in piling the books into the ox-carts.

But even so the Saybrook citizens recapture a certain number of volumes, while others are scattered about the ground. Dr. Daniel Buckingham looks grimly on, yet takes no actual part in the fighting save for giving commands and words of encouragement to the Saybrook men. At last the ox-carts are loaded and turned toward New Haven. They are under guard and still subject to active attack.)

1st Student (*standing on a pile of books*). Victory! I have no Latin to cast the story of this day into a golden epic! I must rejoice in the vulgar tongue!—but did you see me crack that citizen's crown! I vow the buffet will linger in his memory until the January thaw!

2nd Student (*examining his knuckles*). Aye—I did not badly—nunc praesidio impedimentis sumus—.

(*At that moment they are again attacked. The fight grows more violent as they near the broken-down bridge. Nevertheless the ox-carts valiantly ford the stream. During this operation one of them is overturned and spills its entire contents in the brook. The Saybrook citizens utter a shout of triumph. The other carts reach the opposite shore in safety and the pursuit ends. The Saybrook citizens stand upon one shore shaking their fists at the departing New Haveners.*)

Sheriff. Did I not say it would be a bad day's business? But I did my duty as I saw it, praised be! (*He muffles himself gloomily in his cloak again.*) I shall have a stiff back for a fortnight for going abroad in this East wind.

1st Student. Sheriff, thou art one of the seven champions of Christendom!

(*The little cortège passes out, the students following.*)

SCENE IV

THE FIRST COMMENCEMENT
AT NEW HAVEN

By

LEONARD BACON

Before the Rector's House, New Haven. Stupid is revealed, sitting on a bench, working with papers and a lexicon. Enter Clever, singing, followed by Lazy.

Clever.

The leaf of the maple is red again
That flames in the Witches' Wood,
And there is a whisper in my brain,
A tingle in my blood.

My brothers are welcome to all my Greek,
Though it be not a scholar's store.
And save for Horace I care not a leek
If none know Latin more.

Logic how shall I understand,
Or text expound and declare,
If I kiss Mehitabel Chauncey's hand
And see the sun in her hair?

Stupid (from the bench).

Peace! Peace! good Clever! Faith my head spins round.
I founder in the hurricane of sound . . . . . .
I cannot memorize my salutation.

Clever.   Plague take your periods and your peroration!
 (*Singing*) Saith the proverb: To every dog his day,
     So while I have gullet and lungs,
     I'll sing, May the devil carry away
     The Greek and the Roman Tongues.
Stupid (*in despair*).   Ah! What to do!
Clever (*snatching manuscript from him and showing it to Lazy*).   Ha!
    Here's the part I wrote.
    I'll wager that will stick in Stupid's throat
    When he sees the Governor staring with stern eyes
    That seem to sneer at his false quantities.
 (*Singing*) To grammar and syntax I wish bad luck,
    And to all on that path who plod.
    I know a place where a man may pluck
    Blue aster and golden rod.

(*Enter Tutor with Learned at his heel.   Clever ducks behind the bench.*)

Tutor.   For shame, Sir! Singing! And your oration, Sir?
    Not conned yet, from your bearing, I infer.
    Were you religiously convinced, you'd scorn
    To trifle on so serious a morn.
Stupid.   But, Mr. Tutor—
Tutor.   Your time is misapplied.
    Say what you will, the rebuke is justified.
Clever (*re-appearing from behind the bench*).
    If Stupid sang, it was but as the spheres
    Who sing inaudible to Earthly ears.
    And as for singing, Sir, I will be bound
    Men sin not when they make a godly sound.
    And every note that Stupid sang this morn
    Was of a godly tenor, I'll be sworn.
Tutor.   Sir! Sir! So ill a course to vindicate
    Argues your own heart unregenerate.
    Here's Learned now, who has no turn for folly.
Clever.   'Tis not his virtue, but his melancholy.
Tutor.   But he does that his duty leads him to

(*Enter Rector unperceived.*)

YALE COLLEGE

(From an engraving prior to 1750)

Clever. What is that duty which he ought to do?
     Will he save souls by harrying a verb?
     Or curb his passions—who has none to curb—
     By weighing down his spirit with a store
     Of learning coined by better brains before?
     What is it Learned does deserving praise?

Tutor. He—He—

Lazy.   The question's put him in a maze.
     Tutor is staggered. Faith! he's shot his bolt.

Tutor. Peace, shameless insolent!

Learned.   Hold your tongue, you dolt.

Lazy. I'm a dolt, am I? (*Rushes at Learned who shrinks pitiably.*)

Rector.   Faith! he said most true.
     We must find out what Learned ought to do.
     All of man's difficulty is compact
     In the hard question, what shall he enact?
     Let Clever sneer at Learned if he will.
     After the sneer comes the great question still.

Clever. And you perhaps, Sir, know some certain way
     To the right action?

Rector.   Since you ask me, Nay!
     But we begin our search for it to-day.
     Come, gentlemen!

(*Enter from various quarters the Trustees, led by John Davenport; Governor Gurdon Saltonstall, the Honorable William Taylor, Nathan Gold, followed by a few soldiers; Judges and Ministers. A rabble of the Colony throngs in from all quarters.*)

Rector. Salutatorian, commence now your address.

Stupid. Praeses et Socii———Misery and Distress!
     I have forgotten that I had by heart.

Clever. Stupid must always butcher Clever's part.

(*Laughter in the crowd.*)

Rector (*to Clever*). Be silent. It might tax a better head
     Than his or yours to say what should be said.

(*To Taylor.*) Will it please you, Sir, to show us the intent
    Of our benefactor whom you represent.

Taylor (*presenting a paper to Davenport, leader of the Trustees*).
    Take for the College the title and the deed.
    Flourish and grow in light and so God speed.

Davenport (*reading from a paper*). "The trustees of the Collegiate
    School, constituted in the splendid town of New Haven,
    in Connecticut, being enabled by the most generous dona-
    tion of the Honorable Elihu Yale, Esq., to finish the
    College House already begun and erected, gratefully con-
    sidering the honor due to such and so great a benefactor
    and patron, and being desirous in the best manner to
    perpetuate to all ages the memory of so great a benefit
    conferred chiefly on the colony, we the Trustees, having
    the honor of being intrusted with an affair of so great
    importance to the common good of the people, determine
    and ordain that our College House shall be called by the
    name of its munificent patron, and shall be named Yale
    College, that this Province may keep and preserve a last-
    ing monument of such a generous gentleman, who by so
    great a benevolence and generosity, has provided for their
    greatest good, and the peculiar advantage of the inhabi-
    tants both in the present and the future age."

Rector.   It is a noble thing of fair report
    When a man puts forth his strength to a great end.
    Lift up your heads, Ye everlasting gates!
    Oh Empire of the future, who shall call
    Within this portal?   Hence, forth issuing,
    Ruler and ruled together shall create
    In one endeavor the democracy.
    And to that purpose sanctified, elect,
    Rises the University of Light.
    Oh make a joyful noise!

Chorus of Actors.   All gallant men that are alive
    Were born with the strong world to strive.
    Here men of strength shall teach aright
    Our fingers and our hands to fight.

Take up the labor, O endued
With foresight and with fortitude!
And may the spirit here arise
To scatter the Lord's enemies.

The Whole Concourse, Actors and Audience.

Praise God from whom all blessings flow!
Praise him, all creatures here below!
Praise him above, ye heavenly host!
Praise Father, Son, and Holy Ghost!

Facsimile of signature to letter in the possession of the Elizabethan Club

FIRST INTERLUDE

THE PASSING OF THE ARTS AND SCIENCES
FROM THE OLD WORLD TO THE NEW

By

WILLIAM ROSE BENÉT

THE ORDER OF THE INTERLUDE

And now, as though some god should push
Flatly down upon the Sea
A broad-flared bowl, till at its rim
The rising, chafing waves could swim
And (trembling wire-drawn at the lip)
Suddenly slip
With impetuous rush
From every side to fill abrim
That bowl of jade and ivory,—

So in our theatre from all sides
Children troop down like shining tides!
The peacock colors of the Sea
Shimmer undulant in the dancing
Of their vestures swift advancing
From the Bowl's white upper verges. . .
Arts and Sciences variedly,
In vivid robes of shades of red
And purple, mix with these their tread,
Merged in this singing flood are led
Like splendid-costumed slaves—
As though across the westering surges
Of the vast actual Ocean sped
Symbolic figures, through the waves.

And the waves are singing,—hark them sing,
Streaming down and flooding deep,—
All with such rare gifts to bring
The infant Yale, who lies asleep
In the Bowl's green centre there!
Hear their voices thrill the air!

SONG OF THE WAVES

One with the other
Swaying and dancing,
Sister and brother,
See us advancing;
Children of Ocean
Swirling and leaping;
Constant in motion
While you are sleeping!

Hail,
Infant Yale!
We are the waves who assemble and pour you
Gifts of the gods for the future before you.

Moonlight and sunlight
Silver and gild us.
In our green one light
Deeply we build us
Gray realms of mist, or
Green realms of water,
Brother and sister,
Mother and daughter!

Hail,
Infant Yale!
We are the waves that now bear the Immortals
In from the sea through your opening portals!

And from the richer and more stately
Costumed figures, all advancing
Between blue waves and green waves dancing,
There comes another chorus, greatly
Lifting—nobly calling—urging—
Over the manifold waters surging:

SONG OF THE ARTS AND SCIENCES

Music is the breath
Of Immortalis fleet;
Religion conquers Death
And claims the Mercy-Seat;
Art's noble brush and quill
Speak most when death makes still
The hand that gods could guide,
The lips that must repeat
The promptings of their pride!

And Science, in intense
Integrity divine
Wrestles the elements
To find and to refine,
To pierce the clouds of Art
And hearken at the heart
Of Nature and of Death,
Cleave to the straight hard line
And spare nor toil nor breath.

Our magic masters these!
We are slaves at their behest.
We served them on our knees.
We lead them toward the West.
We are Painting, Prose, and Rhyme,
Music, to cling and chime,
Numbers, and Chemistry,—
Physics, to probe and test,—
And rich Philosophy!

Proud-robed as doth befit,
We bear alembic, lyre,
The scrolls of art and wit,
The lamp of quenchless fire,
The judge's hood and mace,
And rule and square to trace
The fact that trains the brain,—
Retort and tube and wire,
Tomes that all things contain.

Thus we descend to you,
Symbols of greater things,
Of realms of thought wherethrough
Ye shall be kings of kings!
Before you, Infant Yale,
You and your splendid Grail,
We gather and lay our choice,
After long journeyings.
LIVE, CONQUER, AND REJOICE!

The figures reach the turf, and stream
From every side, like a mazy dream,
Over the floor of the Bowl—while song
Rises and echoes the walls along.
There on a cradling stone raised high
In the midst, the young child Yale doth lie.
And the waves sweep up tumultuously
Leaping around his throne, and then
Abased and bending ebb back again
While the Arts and Sciences, winding through,
Lay their symbol-gifts on the stone where he
Sleeps so small and wise and new!

And as they withdraw when the rite is done
And weave toward their exits, every one,
The music swimming on the air
Leaves this echo lingering there:

THE POEM

. . . A change came over the sea.
The face of the waters, dim with a dream,
Smiled through the faint dawn wistfully,
Shone in full sunlight splendidly,
And swirled on our world with every stream
Of light to the mind, of hope to the sense,
Flooding on us the imminence
Of wisdom, in all the wave-lights caught
By inspiration, art, or thought
Of older nations.

    Greenly the waters,
Silver the waters flashed and fell
Crowding in from the shrouded deep
With deeds for daylight and dreams for sleep
Where manifold tongues and theories chimed,
Wrangled or rhymed—each like a bell
Prolonging the note of its prophet throat.
Light and bright on the heaving waters,
Swift on the waters Thought's sons and daughters
Danced to their cadenced fall and swell.

In from the sea of mystery,
Waves from the minds that sway that sea,
Out of old kingdoms, warring lands,
Lightly linking sprightly hands,—
Through waves of love and loyalty,
Hope and fear and prophecy,
In to our new democracy
Swift and vigilant Art and Science
Scattered and led their brilliant bands.

So are our genii seen.
From differing deeps they draw.
From the little city Palatine,
Early enduring law;

From Judean Hills, the seed
Whence that great tree has spread
Branching with every sect and creed,
Whose sap is martyr-red;

And here from seas that faint
With sunlight, from the isles,
Perfect beyond rebuke or plaint
Art's self, immortal, smiles—
The torch to Italy,
The trumpet to the North,
The senses' sanctuary.
White art of Greece, stand forth!

Yes, and from Greece, transformed
By the Arabian brain,
Here is the science old knighthood stormed,
That crept and spread through Spain,—
Those dim beginnings won,
Those first conjectures dared,
Till Galileo traced the sun
Copernicus had snared.

Fugitive over the lambently-lighted and salt interfluctant ocean they
    stream
Bearing the fruits of all reason and sturdy revolt, metaphysic emotion
    and dream,
Ideals in the leash of their languages straining, the weapons of welded
    and intimate speech,
The Romance tongues overflowering the Latin, old English enriched
    by the usage of each,—
The Schoolmen's theology mixed with philosophy, striving to blend
    them, and twisted and twined
With footholds prepared for angelic Aquinas in climbing to Heaven,
    but few for Mankind,
Proud Petrarch entranced by the beauty of Hellas, rough Luther with
    Faith grown a sun to his sight

Revealing the evils acrawl in the temple, expedient lying and blasphemous
    blight;

Axe, fagot, and sword, and the sundering of England, with thirty
    years' war o'er the Continent hurled

For creeds,—and a cloud coming over the Princes, a hope for the
    People, a way for the World!

Descartes doubting all, and Spinoza expounding his Infinite Substance,
    and Bacon denying

Assumptions, but searching through Nature,—and Harvey's skilled ear
    to the pulse of our living and dying,

Rapt Kepler unveiling the laws of the heavens, with Newton enlinking
    the great to the small,

Pure chemistry toiling from alchemy's mire through hands of the healers
    to service of all;

Boyle grappling the air and dividing all matter, and Leibnitz and Napier
    number-bemused

In deft mathematics,—the sweep of conjecture's strong current, by
    whirlpool and eddy confused;

The might of all minds brimming up in the cup of wisdom, the hopes
    of all hearts, and the bright

High fervor of poetry, drama and prose, with satire for surgeon and
    love to give light;

The Dreamer of Bedford, Swift's weapon of wonder, vast Milton, with
    Chaucer and Shakspere behind,—

The palette of Flanders, the theatre of Louis, the splendors of Italy
    fresh in the mind!

        Such were the gifts they bore,
        These magian elves from the sea,
        These and a thousand more,
        Our store enduringly.
        Here, where the hard soil flowered
        That infant college, lifts
        Lo, now our many-towered
        Strong casket for these gifts!

        Yes, to us and ours were given,
        Yale, at thy splendid birth,

Dreams that lay hold on Heaven,
Zeal to rebuild the Earth,—
These and a thousand more,
Men's thoughts like couriers flying
Or like ships that beat from shore
After the dream undying!

Treasure unpriced!—as bluely that ocean
Of marvelous waters flashed and fell,
Crowding in from the mystic deep
With deeds for daylight and dreams for sleep,
Showering dowers on faith's devotion,
Calling on builders to build it well
This edifice of a dauntless dream
More than its outer fabrics seem,
A pharos lit on the shores of strife
To reveal in its light immediate life
And send men forth with souls to dare
The deeds that laugh against despair,
Made strong in such faith as made us so
Two hundred years ago!

SECOND OR REVOLUTIONARY EPISODE

SCENE I

THE DEMANDING OF THE KEYS TO THE POWDER HOUSE AND THE MARCH TO CAMBRIDGE, 1775

By

JOHN BALDWIN KENNEDY

(Major, Second Company Governor's Foot Guard)

The Second Company Governor's Foot Guard was organized December 28, 1774. A number of Yale College men were members of the Command at its organization and during the early years of its existence, and many Yale graduates are now in active membership in the Company. The first few months of its early existence were spent in perfecting the organization and in practicing the military exercise. Then came the first call to service.

The news of the Battle of Lexington arrived in New Haven on Friday, the 21st of April, 1775, about noon, and Benedict Arnold, who had been elected the first Captain of the Command, called out his Company and proposed their starting for Lexington to join the American forces. About 50 of the members

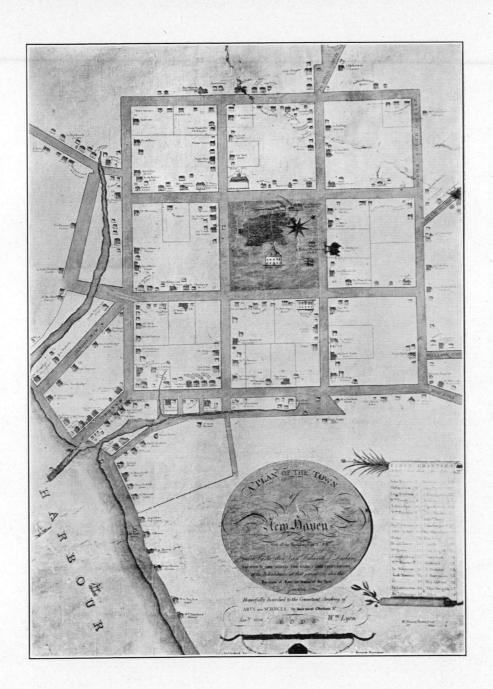

*voted to march on Monday, the 24th of April. Being in need of
ammunition, Captain Arnold requested the town authorities to
furnish the Company with a supply, which they refused to do.
Before starting on their journey, Arnold marched his Company
to the house where the Selectmen were sitting, and, forming them
in front of the building, sent in word demanding supplies.*

Captain Arnold. Lieutenant Leavenworth, you will go to the
room where the Selectmen are sitting and request them to furnish
a supply of powder and ball and flint, from the Town Powder
House, for our Company.

(*Lieutenant Leavenworth salutes and retires.*)

Captain Arnold. Men, we will march to the Green, get our
powder and ball and flint and start on our march.

Lieutenant Leavenworth. Captain Arnold, I report that the
Selectmen refuse to give us any powder, they say that the Colony
has not enough for its own protection, and they further ask why
this great haste. Would it not be better to wait for further
reports from our sister Colony before proceeding?

Captain Arnold. Refuse to give us any powder! Want us to
wait! Do they not see that haste is necessary! Men, do you
hear? We are told to wait; we are told that we can have no
powder. We will have it. We won't wait. Come with me to
the Powder House and we'll supply ourselves.

Men. (*Yells and confused cries of*) Yes, take us to the
Powder House! We will supply ourselves. Lead on! We are
with you. (*A babel of words and cheering.*)

Captain Arnold. Lieutenant Leavenworth, you will say to the
Selectmen that I have received their message that they will not
give us any powder. You will say to them that my Company is
lined up in front ready to march to the assistance of our sister
Colony, and unless they deliver to me the keys to the Powder
House in five minutes, I will order my men to break it open and
supply themselves.

(*Colonel Wooster comes out.*)

Colonel Wooster. Captain Arnold, we admire your spirit and the spirit of the men who are gathered out in front. It is an exhibition of patriotism that will be long remembered in our Colony. We believe that the same spirit exists in all our Colonies, and that this spirit will carry our cause to ultimate victory. Would it not, however, be better to wait for a few days until our General Court, now in session, can appoint the proper officers and see that the regiments, already authorized, are properly assembled, armed and equipped and ready to defend our Colony, or march to the defence of our sister Colony, which is now being attacked?

(*Selectmen come out.*)

Captain Arnold. Colonel Wooster, you know that in this case haste is imperative. Massachusetts has sent for assistance. Let the other troops follow on as soon as possible, but none but God Almighty shall stop me from going to-day. (*Turning to Selectmen.*) Once more I demand the keys.

First Selectman. But this powder is not ours. It belongs to the Colony, and we cannot give it up without a regular order.

Captain Arnold. Regular order be damned! Give it to me or I'll take it!

First Selectman. Captain Arnold, we believe you are acting hastily, but as you are determined to go, rather than have any further unseemly proceedings at this time when all men should stand together, we give you the keys. (*Gives keys to Lieutenant Leavenworth.*)

(*Lieutenant Leavenworth reports to Captain Arnold and salutes.*)

Captain Arnold. Lieutenant, you will take charge of the keys until further orders. Take your post, sir.

(*A detail of men starts off to secure a requisite supply of ammunition. They are approached by one of the ministers of the city, and when, during the ensuing dialogue, the detail which has*

*gone for powder returns with ample supplies, the Company draws
up in full to hear the address of the Reverend Jonathan Edwards,
and, when he has finished, marches off amid the cheers of the
crowd.)*

Minister.   Mr. Captain, I see that you are en route.   There is
an old saying that   "Prayer and provender hinder no journey."
Before you go further, permit me to invite you and your Command to attend divine service.

Captain Arnold.   Reverend Pastor, the old saying is true.   I
heartily accept your bidding in behalf of my Command.

Minister.   God save the Commonwealth of Connecticut.

Captain Arnold.   (*Raising his chapeau.*)   Amen.

It is recorded that Arnold and his men reached Wethersfield
the second night of their march, where the inhabitants of that
town gave them a warm welcome and made them comfortable.
Leaving Wethersfield they took the middle road through Pomfret,
where they were joined by General Israel Putnam.   On their
arrival at Cambridge, they took up their quarters in a mansion
owned by Lieutenant-Governor Oliver of Massachusetts, who had
left on account of his sympathy with the British cause.

The Foot Guard was the only Company on the ground with
complete uniforms and equipment, and owing to their soldier-like
appearance was detailed to deliver to the enemy the body of a
British officer, who had been taken prisoner in the Battle of Lexington and had subsequently died of wounds received in action
in that engagement.   It is said that one of the British officers
appointed to receive the body from the Foot Guard, expressed
surprise at seeing a Company of Americans appear so well in
every respect, observing that, "They were not excelled by any of
His Majesty's troops."   After remaining nearly three weeks at
Cambridge, the Foot Guard (excepting those members who
joined the Continental Army) returned to New Haven.

SCENE II

THE BRITISH INVASION OF NEW HAVEN IN 1779

By

SIMEON EBEN BALDWIN

———————

Sunday evening July 4. Meeting of the citizens in the Center Church. A pulpit and two benches in front of it. Captain Peck occupies the pulpit as Moderator. Citizens are seated on the benches. Among them is Professor Daggett of Yale (Yale 1748) dressed in college cap and gown.

The Moderator. Gentlemen, we have spent over an hour here since candle-light and nothing has been decided except the general vote to have a proper celebration of Independence Day, to-morrow; and to adjourn this meeting at 9 o'clock. It is now nearly nine. I would suggest that some gentleman states what he thinks would be a proper way to celebrate it.

First Citizen. Mr. Moderator, I would suggest that the Declaration of Independence of July 4, 1776, be publicly read in this place, at ten o'clock in the morning.

Second Citizen. Mr. Moderator, there ought to be a salute of cannon, at sunrise.

Third Citizen. Mr. Moderator, we have been rather slow in arranging for this celebration, but there is still time to order a dinner at Mr. Atwater's tavern, for such as choose to pay for it. I should be glad to go for one, and also to subscribe towards the expense of inviting the reverend clergy to join in it.

Fourth Citizen.   It may be our good luck that we have been so slow in finishing up our arrangements.   We really ought to provide for a patriotic address after the reading of the Declaration, and I hear that a likely young man is visiting in town for a few days, who is very good at public speeches.   It is Colonel Aaron Burr of New Jersey, who was on General Putnam's staff in York state.   I move that he be asked to give us an address at the church meeting to-morrow, and respond to a toast at the dinner afterwards, and that all other matters be ordered by a committee of three to be named by the Moderator.

Fifth Citizen.   Mr. Moderator, I second the last motion.

The Moderator.   Gentlemen, are you ready for the question on whether this motion shall pass?   Those in favor will signify it by the uplifted hand.   (*All lift up their hands.*)   The motion is unanimously adopted.   The chair will appoint as the committee of three, the Reverend Professor Daggett, Isaac Beers, and Captain James Hillhouse.   (*Clock strikes nine.*)   The hour has arrived at which it was voted to adjourn this meeting and I declare it adjourned without day.

(*All give three cheers for the United States of America and depart, except the committee of three.*)

Isaac Beers (*addressing Professor Daggett*).   I see, Professor, that you have your cap and gown on.   I thought you did not generally wear them when you were not on official duty.

Professor Daggett.   Sir, I was never more on official duty than at this moment when we are planning to celebrate the Independence of the sovereign State of Connecticut.   She gave the College its charter.   She helped us to build Connecticut Hall.   It is but a poor honor to her, that I should wear this gown and cap on this occasion; but it is the best that I have at my command.   Were I a younger man, I should be in a soldier's coat, in another place.   But it is not given to all to fight for their country, dear as it may be to them.

(*The committee sit down on a bench and confer. An alarm bell is rung. The committee start up. Citizens appear at each of the main gateways, dressed and half dressed. Boys rush in crying,* "Enemy's ships in the harbor!" "British ships off West Haven!" *Captain James Hillhouse appears, on the Green, in front, and some of his military company in Continental uniform of blue and buff. Clock strikes ten. Colonel Burr appears in civilian dress and calls out:* "Where is the first selectman? I must see him immediately."

A signal gun is discharged outside. The citizens gather in groups. Some drive across the Green, to the Northwest, carts laden with furniture.)

Tory Citizen (*addressing Captain Peck.*) Captain, I heard that you were getting up a proper celebration of Independence Day. I congratulate you on your success. It will be numerously attended, you may be sure.

Captain Peck. Sir, I know your sentiments. You are a Tory of the worst kind, Sir, dyed in the wool. Be off, or I will advise the Selectmen to arrest you for aiding and abetting the enemy.

(*The Citizen slinks away.*

Professor Daggett appears, still in academic costume, escorted by a dozen college students, under the command of one of them, George Welles.)

Professor Daggett. Captain Welles, I have come thus far with you, to wish you God speed; you and your company. Young gentlemen, I have tried to teach you something of what they call the humanities of a liberal education. You are now to face the inhumanities of savage invaders. You have a capable and brave commander. I know something of men, and something of him. Follow and obey him; and remember that you are called to fight for your country in an hour of your country's need. I know you will do credit to Yale.

(Two signal guns are discharged. A light artillery company of militia, some in Continental uniform, and some in civilian dress, pass through on their way to East Haven, with their guns. Lieutenant-Colonel Sabin mounts on a box and announces that he takes command of the town. The clock strikes five.

Professor Daggett takes off his cap and gown and gives them to his servant, who has followed him, leading his horse and carrying his musket. More students have now turned out, twenty privates, in all. Colonel Burr appears, mounted and in Continental uniform.)

Colonel Burr. Gentlemen, a proud day has arrived for you and for me. As some of you know, I had the honor until within a few weeks to be a sharer in the defence of our country. I have learned something of military art by the side of those great Connecticut soldiers, General Arnold and General Putnam. Captain Welles, you cannot yourself be present at each of the points where the enemy are likely to attempt an entrance. I know them from observations made here on previous visits. One is Neck Bridge; one the East Haven ferry; another the West Bridge; and another by Hotchkisstown. Lieutenant-Colonel Sabin has done me the honor to make me one of his temporary aides. Will you not, Captain, let me, as representing him, lead a squad of your command to the defence of the town at one of these points?

Captain Welles. It will give me pleasure, Colonel Burr, to put ten men under your command. *(Facing his company.)* "Attention! Shoulder arms! Right dress! Eyes front!" Comrades; ten men are wanted to accompany Colonel Burr, for the purpose you have heard him state. Those ready to volunteer on this service will take one step forward.

(All take one step forward.)

Captain Welles. The first man on the right of the line, and every other man in line will take one step forward.

(Ten men step forward.)

Captain Welles.   Colonel Burr, I have the honor to turn over these men to your command for this day.

(Mounted couriers arrive with dispatches for the selectmen, Colonel Sabin and Colonel Burr, and are dispatched to neighboring towns with news.

Colonel Burr takes the command and leads off his squad, saying to Captain Welles that he shall repair first to Neck Bridge. Captain Welles replies that he will lead the balance of his company to West Bridge and Allingtown. He does so to music of drum and fife, following Captain Hillhouse, who leads off with his company, mostly in Continental uniform.

Professor Daggett rides up and passes them, with a long fowling piece in his hand. They cheer him as he passes. The British appear. Professor Daggett dismounts, ties his horse, and proceeds on foot. He fires his gun at the advanced British scouts. Adjutant Campbell, one of the British Guards, falls and is carried, desperately wounded, into a neighboring house. Captain Hillhouse, Captain Welles, and their commands retreat to West Bridge. As they retreat, Professor Daggett hides in a clump of bushes on the hill. He pokes his gun through the bushes and fires again. A British lieutenant with a squad of men goes to the spot and pulls him out of the bushes, with) :

What are you doing there, you damned old rascal, firing on His Majesty's troops?

Professor Daggett.   I am exercising the rights of war.

Lieutenant.   If I let you go this time, will you ever fire again on the troops of His Majesty?

Professor Daggett.   Nothing more likely.

(Professor Daggett is then dragged down to the head of the British column and driven before it, being pricked occasionally by bayonets to make him keep ahead.

The clock strikes two. A mounted British aide rides ahead, and asks for the town authorities. The first selectman comes forward and is asked if he surrenders the town.)

First Selectman. I do, Sir, for there is no alternative.

(*Citizens, militia, and students now straggle back in disorder, followed soon by the red-coats and Hessians. The latter (the Landgraves) have a uniform of a duller hue. The troops stack arms. General Garth halts and orders his brigade-adjutant to read a Proclamation to the inhabitants. A few citizens gather to hear it. General Tryon accompanies them.*)

PROCLAMATION

"By Commodore Sir George Collier, Commander-in-Chief of His Majesty's ships and vessels in North America, and Major General William Tryon, commanding His Majesty's land forces on a separate expedition.

ADDRESS TO THE INHABITANTS OF CONNECTICUT

"The ungenerous and wanton insurrection against the sovereignty of Great Britain, into which this colony has been deluded by the artifices of designing men, for private purposes, might well justify in you every fear which conscious guilt could form, respecting the intentions of the present armament.

"Your towns, your property, yourselves, lie within the grasp of the power whose forbearance you have ungenerously construed into fear; but whose lenity has persisted in its mild and noble efforts, even though branded with the most unworthy imputation.

"The existence of a single habitation on your defenceless coast ought to be a subject of constant reproof to your ingratitude. Can the strength of your whole province cope with the force which might at any time be poured through every district in your country? You are conscious it cannot. Why then will you persist in a ruinous and ill-judged resistance? We hoped that you would recover from the phrenzy which has distracted this unhappy country; and we believe the day to be near come when the greater part of this continent will begin to blush at their delusion. You who lie so much in our power, afford the most striking monument of our mercy, and therefore ought to set the first example of returning allegiance.

"Reflect on what gratitude requires of you; if that is insufficient to move you, attend to your own interest; we offer you a refuge against the distress which, you universally acknowledge, broods, with increasing and intolerable weight over all your country.

"Leaving you to consult with each other upon this invitation, we do now declare, that whoever shall be found and remain in peace, at his usual place of residence, shall be shielded from any insult, either to his person, or his property, excepting such as bear offices, either civil or military, under your present usurped government, of whom it will be further required that they shall give proofs of their penitence and voluntary submission; and they shall then partake of the like immunity.

"Those whose folly and obstinacy may slight this favorable warning, must take notice, that they are not to expect a continuance of that lenity which their inveteracy would now render.

"Given on board His Majesty's ship Camilla, on the Sound, July 4, 1799.

GEORGE COLLIER,
WM. TRYON."

(*Printed copies are distributed.*)

General Garth.   Adjutant, has the proclamation of freedom to all slaves who join us been already read?

Adjutant.   Yes, Sir, it was read on landing at Union Wharf; and will be read again there, when we re-embark.

Colonel Edmund Fanning (*in command of one of the invading regiments, stepping forward, and addressing General Garth*). General, on your left are the buildings of Yale College.   I am an alumnus of Yale of the Class of 1757.   If the town should be burned, I venture to ask that these buildings be spared.

General Garth.   Whether the town is burned or not, whether in whole or part, must depend upon General Tryon.

General Tryon.   Thus far no resistance has been made since the surrender of the town.   Colonel Fanning's intercession shall be considered later.   We shall not forget that we have many friends here.

(British wounded pass through the town. The American prisoners march up under guard. Among them is Professor Daggett, who stumbles along with difficulty. Two of the Hessians, who are on the Green, slip off and desert. Joshua Chandler (Yale 1747), a Tory lawyer, steps up to the commander of the guard over the prisoners, and obtains permission for the release of Professor Daggett on account of his feeble condition. The Professor is carried off on a litter.

The clock strikes nine, the British troops form. Colonel Fanning rides up to General Garth.)

Colonel Fanning. General, may I hope that my old college town will not be burned?

General Garth. The orders are not to burn it, Sir. It is too beautiful a town to burn.

(Evacuation. The British troops form and march out, with a brass band. The prisoners, thirty or forty, follow. Between two of the regiments are some thirty Tory Americans, carrying small trunks, portmanteaus, and bundles, on the way to take ship and abandon their country. Mr. Chandler is among them, and the citizen who jeered at Captain Peck.)

SCENE III

THE MARTYRDOM OF NATHAN HALE

By

GEORGE DUDLEY SEYMOUR

"That life is long which answers life's great end."—Young.

It is a Sabbath morning, and the place the encampment of the Royal Artillery overlooking the East River, and facing the Old Post Road from New York to Albany and Boston, not far from the spot where Hale's regiment had landed but a few months before. The parade ground of the camp is empty save for a small straggling group of old men, women and children, and a thin line of red-coated soldiers. To the South, a cloud of smoke rises from the burning city of New York, half obscuring the sky and casting its pall of gloom over the scene of the tragedy about to be enacted. In the distance, the grave and even agonizing sound of muffled drums is heard with smiting reverberations. Gradually these increase in intensity until two drummers appear, followed by a rude cart dragged along by half a dozen unkempt soldiers, hardly recognizable as such in their rough undress. Behind them the common hangman, a mulatto, bears the ladder, his neck, as was the grewsome custom, encircled by the fatal rope. Then a handful of soldiers in uniform, marching two by two, and beside them, the British Provost Marshal Cunningham, drunken, ferocious, and of an infamy so notorious that the by-standers shrink back from him. And then,—Hale—his hands bound behind him, walking alone, with measured tread—a Captain in the Continental Army, and yet so boyish, with flushed cheeks

THE EXECUTION OF NATHAN HALE

(From an illustration in Stuart's *Life of Captain Nathan Hale*)

and fair hair.   He is of medium height, but the quiet dignity
of his bearing, the freedom of his carriage, and his high color,
give him a certain brightness which lifts him above the rest
of the company.   Looking straight forward, he moves to his
fate.   Once he raises his handsome head to note the great pillar
of smoke rising from the burning city and doubtless wonders at
the portent of the conflagration.   He hears with no outward sign
of emotion the half stifled cries of the women and children who
watch his forward march to the beat of those muffled drums.
Simply and quietly he walks to his doom, thinking, perchance, of
the broad landscape of his boyhood home beyond the Eastern
hills in Coventry, of Connecticut Hall where he spent so many
happy hours, of the loved home circle and his friends.   We can
imagine him unflinching without, but tremulous within—he was
young, life was dear to him, the earth that he looked upon was
fair, friendship had been sweet to him, he did not wish to die.—
A few more soldiers in worn and faded uniforms follow with
stolid faces and remonstrant hearts, and lastly, at one side, with
bowed head and slow stride, the gallant and noble figure of Captain Montresor, who alone of that company had befriended
Hale during the morning hours when the preparations were being
made for the final scene.   This little cortège passes before us and
makes us feel, as never before, the rhythm and meaning of that
sad lyric:—

> To drum-beat and heart-beat,
> A soldier marches by;
> There is color in his cheek,
> There is courage in his eye,
> Yet to drum-beat and heart-beat,
> In a moment he must die.*

Slowly the procession disappears and leaves the parade ground
empty except for the little group of stragglers who may not enter

---

* From the poem by Francis Miles Finch, Yale 1849, read at the centennial anniversary of the Linonia Society, July 27, 1853.

the orchard to witness the end. The drum-beats grow fainter
and fainter, and die away into a terrifying silence. * * *
* * * The tolling of a bell announces that all is over—that
the tragedy is complete. Hale has "resigned his life a sacrifice
to his country's liberty." We almost hear whispered above us,
in the stillness of the vacant air, descending as a precious legacy
upon us, the youthful patriot's now immortal last words,—"I only
regret that I have but one life to lose for my country."

HISTORICAL NOTE

The above Scene, as arranged for presentation, is founded
mainly on the account given by Captain Montresor a day or two
after the event, to Captain William Hull (Yale 1772), Hale's
close friend and companion in arms, who had endeavored to dis-
suade him from his perilous undertaking. Stuart's "Life," published 1856, has also been drawn upon for some of the details.

Hull's account, as given in his Memoirs, is as follows:—

I learned the melancholy particulars from this officer, (Montresor)
who was present at his execution, and seemed touched by the circumstances attending it.

He said that Captain Hale had passed through their army, both of
Long Island and York Island. That he had procured sketches of the
fortifications, and made memoranda of their number and different
positions. When apprehended, he was taken before Sir William Howe,
and these papers, found concealed about his person, betrayed his intentions. He at once declared his name, his rank in the American army,
and his object in coming within the British lines.

Sir William Howe, without the form of a trial, gave orders for his
execution the following morning. He was placed in the custody of
the Provost Marshal, who was a Refugee, and hardened to human
suffering and every softening sentiment of the heart. Captain Hale,
alone, without sympathy or support, save that from above, on the near
approach of death asked for a clergyman to attend him. It was refused.
He then requested a Bible; that too was refused by his inhuman jailer.

"On the morning of his execution," continued the officer, "my station was near the fatal spot, and I requested the Provost Marshal to

permit the prisoner to sit in my marquee, while he was making the necessary preparations. Captain Hale entered; he was calm, and bore himself with gentle dignity, in the consciousness of rectitude and high intentions. He asked for writing materials, which I furnished him; he wrote two letters, one to his mother and one to a brother officer." He was shortly after summoned to the gallows. But a few persons were around him, yet his characteristic dying words were remembered. He said, "I only regret that I have but one life to lose for my country."

The most detailed account of Hale's personal appearance which has come down to us, is that contained in the pungent reminiscences written by Lieut. Elisha Bostwick, of New Milford, on his Commission (signed by John Hancock), now on file in the Revolutionary War Pension Archives at Washington. It was the writer's good fortune to rediscover this document at Washington some two years ago. Of Hale, Bostwick writes *con amore:*—

I will now make some observations upon the amiable & unfortunate Capt. Nathan Hale whose fate is so well known; for I was with him in the same Regt. both at Boston & New York & until the day of his tragical death; & although of inferior grade in office was always in the habits of friendship & intimacy with him; & my remembrance of his person, manners & character is so perfect that I feel inclined to make some remarks upon them; for I can now in imagination see his person & hear his voice—his person I should say was a little above the common statute in height, his shoulders of a moderate breadth, his limbs straight & very plump; regular features—very fair skin—blue eyes—flaxen or very light hair which was always kept short—his eyebrows a shade darker than his hair and his voice rather sharp or piercing—his bodily agility was remarkable. I have seen him follow a football & kick it over the tops of the trees in the Bowery at New York (an exercise which he was fond of)—his mental powers seemed to be above the common sort—his mind of a sedate and sober cast, & he was undoubtedly Pious; for it was remarked that when any of the soldiers of his company were sick he always visited them & usually prayed for & with them in their sickness.—

A little anecdote I will relate; one day he accidentally came across some of his men in a bye place playing cards—he spoke—what are you doing—this won't do,—give me your cards, they did so, & he chopd them to pieces, & it was done in such a manner that the men were rather pleased than otherwise—his activity on all occasions was wonderful— he would make a pen the quickest, & the best of any man— x x x x x One more reflection I will make—why is it that the delicious Capt. Hale should be left & lost to an unknown grave & forgotten!—

Through the eyes of Bostwick, we have seen Hale as he looked to his comrades in arms; Hull has preserved for us Montressor's impression of Hale in the hour of his sacrifice.

A brief sketch of Hale's short life and we must part from him. Nathan Hale was born at Coventry, Connecticut, June 6th, 1755, the fourth son and sixth child of the twelve children of Deacon Richard Hale, an energetic farmer, a man of sturdy character and public spirit. On both sides the inheritance was of the best old New England stock. He was prepared for college by the village minister and entered Yale in 1769 with the Class of 1773. It is plain from the evidence at hand that he was one of the foremost figures in his Class. His engaging personality, serious mindedness, skill as an athlete, and his ardent temperament, made him a marked man in the college world of his time. He was one of the chief supporters and a strong partisan of Linonia and assisted Tutor Dwight in building up its library. We have no more interesting and attractive picture of fraternity life at Yale than we get through the fading minutes of the Linonia Society now preserved in the College Library, and partly written in Hale's own clear and even elegant hand. After graduation in 1773, he taught school in East Haddam for a few months, leaving there in March, 1774, to become the preceptor of the Union Grammar School in New London, where he was teaching when the war broke out. Ardently patriotic, he enlisted and served as First Lieutenant in a Connecticut Regiment throughout the Siege of Boston. In March, 1775, he went with his regiment to New York and served there until his untimely end, meanwhile having been commissioned a Captain in the Continental Army.

In responding to Washington's call in September, 1776, for information of the enemy's strength and position, he seems to have been fully conscious of the danger of his undertaking. He started on his hazardous mission about September 12th, crossing the Sound at Norwalk. Nothing is known of his experiences in the enemy's lines, and no satisfactory account of the place and mode of his capture has yet appeared. He was executed in New York on Sunday morning, September 22nd, 1776—one hundred and forty years ago. It is hard for us now to realize that he was only in his twenty-second year, having passed his twenty-first birthday on the 6th of the previous June. Recent researches by Professor Johnston place his execution at about the intersection of Third Avenue and 65th or 66th Streets.

Hale had many friends in the Continental Army, and his general and college acquaintance was wide. The neglect of his memory by those who should have cherished it and paid tribute to him is only explained by the ignominy that attached to the mode of his death. Even in his own home his name was not spoken— so sharp was the feeling that the family had been disgraced by having a member of it hanged as a spy. Barring the living, to-day Nathan Hale is probably the best known American, after Washington and Lincoln, and the best known of all Yale men. It is a cause for thankfulness that after comparative neglect for a century, he should now have definitely taken his place as our youthful national hero, and our matchless symbol of patriotism. In his youth, in his personal beauty and athletic prowess, in his simplicity and straightforwardness of character, in his supreme sacrifice and early death, he has an unfading brightness which must forever endear him to all who are quick to feel a modest and manly spirit.

SCENE IV

PRESIDENT WASHINGTON'S VISIT
TO NEW HAVEN IN 1789

By

HOWARD MANSFIELD

During the half year following his inauguration in New York
on April 30, 1789, President Washington devoted himself to the
task of organizing the new government. Having first chosen,
with rare and impartial judgment, a cabinet of efficient advisers,
he next addressed himself to the selection of the justices of the
Supreme Court. In this he was able to bring together representative lawyers of notable ability from various sections, with the
obvious purpose of insuring respect throughout the country for
decisions which might well be anticipated to arouse local criticism
and objection. The work of shaping governmental policies which
should accord with the framework of the newly adopted constitution and become the dignity of the young republic, combined with
the perplexing task of filling minor offices, taxed severely Washington's energies, and he suffered a serious illness in August. In
spite of this, he brought his preliminary labors to a pause at the
end of September, when Congress took a recess.

Throughout the intervening period, one predominant purpose
appears from numerous evidences to have been kept by Washington steadily in mind, and that was that the office of President
of the United States should command the highest respect both
at home and abroad. It was partly to emphasize the national
significance of this office that Washington, in October, 1789,
started on his first official visit to New England, proceeding, by

A Front VIEW of YALE-COLLEGE, and the COLLEGE CHAPEL, New-Haven.

A compendious History of Yale-College, and a general Account of the Course of Studies pursued by the Students.

YALE-COLLEGE was founded
A. D. 1700, and flourishes to this
day.

way of New Haven, Hartford, Worcester, Boston, Salem, and Newburyport, as far as Portsmouth, New Hampshire. He was absent about a month and returned by a different route through the interior as far as Hartford. On his return he reached New Haven on the afternoon of November the tenth, merely remaining for the night and setting out early next morning for New York.

It was, therefore, not as General Washington but as President Washington that he traversed the new States that had been so zealous for their colonial rights; not all of their group yet under the new constitution, nor all yet surely convinced that a central controlling government had come into being. He traveled from city to city in his own carriage, accompanied by his two secretaries, Mr. Lear and Mr. Jackson.

Everywhere the old loyalty and the personal affection with which Washington was greeted on his journey in 1775 to take command of the Continental forces at Cambridge, were renewed, strengthened inevitably by appreciation of the character and fortitude that had so conspicuously brought success to the cause of liberty and independence. As General he had been enthusiastically welcomed at New Haven in 1775 by the citizens of the town and by the Yale students, who, with Noah Webster at their head playing the flute, had escorted well on his way the commander on whom their hopes were centered. As President he was welcomed there with like enthusiasm and equal confidence, but with more ceremony, in 1789. He reached the city on Saturday, October the seventeenth, a date corresponding to that on which his entry is to be celebrated in the Pageant of 1916, commemorating the establishing of Yale College in New Haven. The session of the College was not to begin until the following Tuesday, but it may be assumed that the undergraduates, as well as the members of the new class, were already in the town for so notable an occasion.

At this time, New Haven, which had been incorporated on January 21, 1784, was a city of about four thousand inhabitants out of a population of less than ten thousand within the limits of a town covering a much larger territory. The College numbered some eighty-eight members of the three upper classes, while, as recorded in the Diary of the Reverend Doctor Ezra Stiles, then President of the College, thirty-three were in waiting to become members of the new class.

From the narrative in the *Connecticut Journal* of October 21, 1789, quoted in the *History of the City of New Haven,* edited by Edward E. Atwater, New York, 1887, it appears that "having received information of the approach of the President of the United States of America," the House of Representatives appointed Mr. Edwards, Governor Griswold, Mr. Tracy, Major Hart, Mr. Dana, Mr. Larned, Mr. Ingersoll, Colonel Seymour, Colonel Leffingwell, Colonel Grosvenor, and Mr. Davenport, "with such gentlemen as the Honorable Council shall join, a committee to prepare and report an address from this Legislature to the President of the United States, on his arrival in this city, and to meet the President at some convenient distance from said city, and attend him to his lodgings, and to present such address as shall be ordered, and to attend the President on his journey as far as propriety shall in their opinion require." In the Upper House, Mr. John Chester and Mr. James Hillhouse were appointed to join the Committee of the House of Representatives. It further appears that "the Legislature also requested his Excellency, the Governor, to order his company of guards in this city to attend the Committee in escorting the President."

The published narrative of the events of the day includes the address to the President from the Legislature, signed by Samuel Huntington, Governor, and the address from the Congregational ministers of the City of New Haven, signed by Ezra Stiles, James Dana, Jonathan Edwards, Samuel Wales, and Samuel Austin, Jun., and Washington's replies to these addresses. The narrative adds: "The next day he attended Divine Service in Trinity Church. His Excellency the Governor, his Honor the Lieutenant-Governor, Hon. Roger Sherman, the Honorable the Speaker of the House of Representatives, with the Treasurer, dined with him; and attended the afternoon service at the Rev. Dr. Edwards'

Meeting." The narrative ends: "Early on Monday morning the President set out from hence for the Eastern States."

* * * * * * * * * * *

For the Pageant the ceremonies of the day are presented as taking place on the Green, east of Temple Street. The President, having left his lodgings with the military escort, enters from the corner of Church and Chapel Streets by the road that then crossed the Green diagonally to the corner of College and Elm Streets.

Summoned by the joyous ringing of church bells, the citizens in great numbers and in holiday attire are gathered to greet him. The undergraduates of Yale College, who have come back for the occasion in advance of the opening of the college year, are present on the scene wearing their caps and gowns, and with them are the candidates for admission. The flag of the new nation is everywhere displayed with the banner of the new State of Connecticut. Triumphal arches adorned with branches of brilliant autumnal foliage have been erected, and, as the President approaches, his pathway under the arches is strewn with garlands by gaily dressed maidens.

His approach is heralded by the firing of the presidential salute, and he is received with every mark of honor and affection and a universal outburst of patriotic fervor. His guard of honor is the Second Company of Governor's Foot Guards, under the command of Captain William Lyon, and is preceded by its drum and fife corps playing martial music. The President enters, in civilian dress, on a white horse, accompanied by his secretaries and attended by the Governor of the State, in civilian dress, and the Governor's staff, in appropriate uniforms; all on horseback. On halting, after passing through the triumphal arches, the President is met by the Lieutenant-Governor, Oliver Wolcott, the Speaker of the House of Representatives, Pierpoint Edwards, the State Treasurer, Jedidiah Huntington, and the Committee of the Legislature, on whose behalf Mr. James Davenport, Clerk of the House of Representatives, and Mr. George Wyllys, Secretary of the

Upper House, present the address of welcome from the Legislature, which the President receives and to which he makes a reply, amid great applause.

Another address is presented by President Stiles of the College, specially representing a group of six Congregational ministers, who, with the students, are gathered about him. To this address also the President replies. Following renewed applause, the students sing "Gaudeamus," and the scene becomes one of unbounded enthusiasm, the students leading in cheers for the President.

After the brief ceremonies are over, the martial music strikes up again, and the President, with the Governor and his staff and the guard of honor, proceeds across the Green, acknowledging with evident appreciation the continuous greetings of the assembled citizens. The students separate and form a lane through which the procession passes, and then, closing their ranks, follow as an escort, cheering and waving flags.

President Stiles and the ministers depart toward the College; the officers of the General Assembly and the members of the Legislative Committee retire, and the citizens disperse in different directions with demonstrations of continuing enthusiasm.

SECOND INTERLUDE

AN ALLEGORY OF WAR AND PEACE

By

FRANCIS HARTMAN MARKOE

First there shall be silence, and then a low long wailing cry, as if the hearts of all the world were breaking. Then a weary restless music with long disordered rhythm, and the sounds of uneasy things stirring and moaning, and the while, coming into the Bowl, the Little Spirits of Starved Desire and Fear of Brotherhood. They drift hither and whither like efts in an uncomprehended stream. The music grows wilder, and they mass here and there in seething circles, malicious ganglia of mischief. Suddenly with black-smoking torches appear the warped souls of Demagogues and Self-lovers, whose eyes are too puny to see beyond themselves.

The Wise Voice of the Old, Deep, Unchanging World:

> War!
> The Chaos of Will,
> The fruit of Desire—
> Washing the land with the smoke
> Of its holocaust fire—
> As the forest-flames on the hills,
> When the summer drought
> Has sapped the life of the trees,
> Belch out
> Their scorching breath

To ravish the dying green,
War!
Unleashed on the too serene
Stagnating life of a nation
Parched with prosperous years,
Vomits its desolation.
War!
From whose horrible maw
Of hideous pain
Are spewed forth,
In the cud of despair,
The regurgitate waste
Of our hopes, dreams, and need;
Yet who brings
Like a Phoenix in throes of new birth
From her fire of death, a fresh Earth
And old Heaven revital in truth.

(The vortex grows wilder. Chaos is complete. Suddenly from all sides appear the Hierodules of War, the glad holy servants of its sacrifice. First advancing come the Young Men Who Have Found Their Manhood.)

Beloved, best beloved,
We come at last
The glad bridegrooms.
Now all the weary empty-time is past,
The time of faint desire and undefined ambitions.
As the light plane, the wings and rudder set,
When the propeller beats against the air,
Tugs at the human leashes
And then skims the ground,—
Rises, skims, rises,—
The freeing air
Once caught beneath its wings,—rises—
So we break through dead arms,
Leave little love behind, leave pain of parting
And desire for greeting, and leaping

Lose ourselves into the blue—
Beloved, best beloved,
We come at last.
Beloved,
Best beloved!

(As they go forward there is a sound as of a whirlwind of wings above their heads and the voices of the Contented Dead sing to them):

All the dreams that were sweet in dreaming
Are sweeter yet when laid aside,
And the satisfaction of life's achievement
Is only for those who have nobly died.
Youth, ease, hope, love, unborn children,
Fine ambition, strength in strife,
Fall as dust from the feet of a runner.
He only gains, who loses, life.

(Then come the Mothers to whom for their greater glory the purest pain in the world is given, sad, grey-clad figures with their men-children at their sides.)

We are the mothers;
Ours was the pain
Of bearing men
And now again
Of losing them.
Ours were the dreams
When the hope of the world lay within us.
Ours were the fears for the future,
Ours were the teaching years.
Ours is the hopeless future,
Ours the desolate home,
The vacant chair, the empty world,
The twilight-whispered name.

(As they go forward towards the altar with their sons, there is the sound of a mighty earthquake, and again as of evening sunlight and morn-clear when the eyes see beyond the limits of vision.)

The cry of the soil is the cry of the mother,
All things have their part in the pains of birth;
The broken dream and love torn asunder
Are the paths to God and the purge of Earth.

(Then come Life's Wastrels, deep-eyed and world-sick, but unrepentant, because in the gall they drink is the true understanding of others' misery, the essential oil of shared pity.)

We who were wasters and wanton,
Weary, dreary, and damned,
Sick with self-comprehension,
With the dross of the things we shammed,
Now we find resurrection,
Wiping our old scores down,
Now for doing, not meaning,
The old indecision's gone.
Gone with ceaseless yearning,
Gone with black bitterness,
With tired thought, abused body,
And specious-gay mirthlessness.
At last the sun is glorious,
The clear star-lit night-air sweet,
Eyes, fearing no others, meet.
Joyous, clean, free all the hours,
We are men,
Shall die men,
Have lived men!
Redemption is ours!

(As they go forward from an infinite distance off, as though it were the sound of summer clouds singing together, is heard):

Sanctus, Sanctus,
Sanctus, Sanctus,
Sanctus, Sanctus,
Dominus Deus.

(While from the nearer ether sounds):

The law of despair and the sword
Is the law of the sun and the star,
The law of womb-birth and of love.
All things work together for good
To them that love God.

(Then follow Noble Wives with little children at their breasts, bravely smiling farewell to their husbands; Old Men ready and glad to give up their dreamed of old age; Calm Fathers with their only sons, and a host of Other Heroic, Patriot Hearts, while above the riot sound ever nearer and near the Hymning Voices):

Sanctus, Sanctus,
Sanctus, Sanctus,
Sanctus, Sanctus,
Dominus Deus.

(Then suddenly in an instant the wild clamor is hushed. There is a moment's silence, and then a thin white sound, glad as the dancing of sunlight on rippling waters, fills the air. It laughs, throbs, lilts, and flows, like the summer sea on long sand beaches, or little winds on August wheat fields. And Peace is there. Radiant, majestic, glowing, with little children playing about her, she advances quietly towards the altar and the air is filled with the scent of ineffable flowers.

The Rout of War fall back from the altar, which they have before hidden, disclosing thereon a wan, emaciated, hollow-eyed, blood-bruised little child, the youngest and oldest thing in the world, who stretches out her thin, tired arms toward Peace):

Sanctus, Sanctus,
Sanctus, Sanctus,
Sanctus, Sanctus,
Dominus Deus,

(*sound the Voices in ecstasy, while Peace folds her into her bosom
where with a little tired sob, having done her worst and her best,
she nestles to rest.*

Then the air is rent with a great shout):

Evoë! Evoë!
Laugh! the winter of war is sped!
Sing! summer and sun-glad the hours!
Peace comes! The graves of the dead
Are covered with flowers!
Evoë! Evoë!

(*And brimming over the rim of the Bowl pour down from all
sides the Processions of Peace. First the hours of Youth,
Dawn, and Spring, waving blossoming branches and singing*):

Spring, Spring, Spring, Spring!
Every branch is burgeoning.
Now the sun with the dawn
Gilds the fresh green of the lawn,
Where grass-blade vies with clover
In the turf's thick new cover.
Winter's deadlock strike is over,
Bees and birds and plants and men
All are busy once again,
For labour loved's but holiday!
Bind our brows then with arbutus,
Laughter-strong who dare dispute us
Regal rights of vernal sway?

(Next the aureate hours of Summer, Day, and Growth, with golden laurel boughs):

Sing, bird! whisper, tree!
Winds, make melody!
Summer's here, hearts are free.
Mates wait each wight's choosing,
Love's gain's Love's losing.
Phlox, stocks, and hollyhocks
Fill the garden's fragrant borders;
Gold alyssum on the rocks
Lures the miser honey-hoarders,
With dim dianthus' misty stars,
Most humble yet most sweet of flowers,
And fragile fuchsia bells that ring
The churching summer and knell of spring.
Harvests ripen and grow mellow,
Branches bend with fragrant fruit,
While the sun feeds the fallow
The cicada's throbbing note
Thrills through field and meadow;
And where the water-fern's green fronds
Fringe the lily-padded ponds
Iridescent dragon flies
Catch the setting orb's last rays.

(And last the soft hours of Evening, Autumn, and Completion):

Long shadows soothe the wide-flung hills to sleep,
Rosaureate horizons melt gold to grey,
Day's intimate sky recedes to night's far fields
Where browsing star-flocks pasture, and the scent
Of dusk-sweet flowers from the garden blows.
Twittering the swallows wing about the eaves,
The ghosts of garnered harvests haunt the weald.
Oh sweet to rest long evenings after toil,
Safe housed and happy, when tomorrow holds
No tragedy except of falling leaves!

(*When the Processions of the Glory of Peace have passed down the steps and into the Bowl, they advance to where Peace stands and, kneeling before her, hold out their offerings for her benediction, while from above sounds once more, glorious and triumphant*):

Sanctus, Sanctus,
Sanctus, Sanctus,
Sanctus, Sanctus,
Dominus Deus Sabaoth.
Pleni sunt caeli et terra gloria tua,
Hosanna in excelsis.
Amen.   Amen.

(*After this they rise and turn outwards to bear the Joy of Peace to the world, and as they pass upward, they sing*):

Ecce nunc, benedicite Dominum, omnes servi Domini.
Magna opera Domini: exquisita in omnes voluntas ejus.
Quis sicut Dominus Deus noster, qui in altis habitat: et
    humilia respicit in coelo et in terra?
Non nobis, Domine, non nobis: sed nomini tuo da gloriam.
A facie Domini mota est terra: a facie Dei Jacob.
Qui convertit petram in stagna aquarum: et rupen in fontes aquarum.
In pace in idipsum dormiam, et requiescam.
Quoniam tu, Domine, singulariter in spe constituisti me.
Per omnia saecula saeculorum
Pax Domini sit semper nobiscum.

THE END OF THE ALLEGORY

THIRD OR EARLY NINETEENTH CENTURY EPISODE

SCENE I

TOWN AND GOWN RIOT

By

HENRY AUGUSTIN BEERS

The Pageant presents a sort of composite photograph of the three famous encounters of 1841, 1854, and 1858, without regard to strict historical accuracy. The antagonism of *Bursch* and *Philister* —airs of superiority on the one side, with jealousy and resentment on the other—is as old as universities themselves. The tales of the *Clerici vagantes* in the Middle Ages, illustrated in English by Chaucer's "Reeves Tale" and "Milleres Tale," testify to the antiquity of the dispute.

At Yale, though there were doubtless earlier and unrecorded hostilities, the first Town and Gown rows of importance seem to have broken out in the last years of the eighteenth and the first years of the nineteenth centuries, when students resorting to a certain tavern in "Dragon," or Fair Haven, got into a fight with the oystermen, sailors, and similar native frequenters of the place. These battles were continued, or resumed, at Long Wharf; where students went to bathe and were attacked by mariners, longshoremen, wharf-rats, and the miscellaneous water-side population. In one of these encounters occurred the winning of that Excalibur, the celebrated Bully Club, said to have been

wrested from the grasp of a pirate by Asa Thurston of the Class
of 1818, a quondam blacksmith of peaceable disposition but enormous strength; and, like Posson Jone, a "so fighting an' moz
rilligious man."

Somewhat later the storm center appears to have shifted from
the Dragonites to the volunteer fire companies of New Haven,
which had a strong *esprit de corps* and included a considerable
rowdy element. The Southern students, who were then numerous in the college, were quick in quarrel, and many of them
went armed with pistols or knives. The affairs of 1841 and 1858
were affairs between the students and firemen, the latter between
members of the Crocodile Club and of Engine No. 2, in which
William Miles, a fireman, was shot dead. But the fire companies
were not particularly concerned in the pitched battle of 1854, in
which South College, where the students had barricaded themselves, was besieged all night by an angry mob, and two cannon
trained upon the building. That affair began in a row at a theatre—the college men were followed all the way up Chapel Street
by a crowd of "townies," and assailed with stones and brick-bats,
until their leader, Patrick O'Neil, a barkeeper and general tough,
was stabbed through the heart by a dirk in the hand, it was said,
of a Senior from Mississippi.

Our scene presents the southwestern corner of the city Green.
The annual football game between the Sophomores and Freshmen
is in progress. There are about a hundred men on each side,
mostly bare-headed and in shirt-sleeves, in old clothes, and some
in purposely grotesque costumes. There was nothing scientific
about the game: the picture is of "a dense mass of men, shouting, shoving, dragging, struggling, swaying to and fro toward
either side of the field." There is holding, slugging, shin-kick-
ing; men grab each other by the throat or the hair. Now and
then the ball, a pig's bladder covered with leather, soars above the
crowd. Cries of "Hi! Forty-four! Forty-five! Stop him!
Quick! This way! Hold him! Push! Get the ball! Let go
my hair, you damn Freshman!"

EASTERN VIEW OF THE PUBLIC SQUARE OR GREEN, IN NEW HAVEN, CONN.

FROM A VIEW TAKEN IN 1840

To these enter, from different sides, several fire companies, about fifty men in all, in red shirts and helmets, the captains calling orders through brass speaking trumpets. One company drags its hose across the football field, *en route* toward Center Church, where the companies will compete in playing on the spire. The game is broken up and turns into a free fight between students and firemen. Cries of "Yale! Yale! Cut the hose! Send for the Bully Club!" And on the opposite side, "Town! Town! Hustle the monkeys! This way, Hose Company No. 3! Get off the Green, ye damn stewed-nuts!" The ball is seized by the enemy—the hose is cut in a dozen places. The Bully Club, a gnarled oaken club, appears in the van, wielded by Hezekiah Sturges, '41, the last Bully. Three students (including Thomas Hudson Moody, '43, of Georgia) are finally arrested by the firemen, who constitute themselves a constabulary force and escort their prisoners toward the lower end of the Green, on the way to the police station. The students form a rescue party and attack the rear of the procession with cries of "Yale! Yale! Come on, fellows! Get our men loose!" There are scrimmages, several shots are fired—a fireman drops dead. Pause. The students gradually retire toward the colleges. The crowd about the center increases rapidly, and includes, besides the firemen, sympathizing citizens and unclassified "townies" of all kinds. A group of firemen appears from somewhere dragging a cannon. The crowd swarm about it and rush it up to College Street with shouts of "Bring out the murderer! Blow up the college! Give 'em hell, boys!" A squad of policemen fight their way to the cannon and succeed in spiking it. The mayor of the city comes upon the scene, gets astride the cannon, and makes a speech to the infuriated mob. He takes off his hat, waves his arms, and makes signs for the crowd to disperse, but his voice is lost in the uproar. The students have all disappeared, the cannon has been put out of business, and the mob slowly and sullenly melts away, carrying off the dead and wounded.

SCENE II

THE BURIAL OF EUCLID

By

ARTHUR COLTON

HISTORICAL SKETCH

The origin of the *Burial of Euclid,* meaning the date of it, is unknown, but in 1843 it was said to be "handed down from time immemorial." The origin, meaning the circumstances which lay back of, gave rise to and continued to maintain it, was in general, of course, the natural attitude of youth toward alien authority, and in particular the great unpopularity of Freshman and Sophomore mathematics. There is other evidence than the records of this ritual for the intensity and persistence of this feeling. The classes of 1827 and 1832 mutinied against their mathematical oppressors, to the result that half of the Class of '27 was suspended, and forty-four of the Class of '32, out of a total membership of ninety, were expelled. The hostility continues noticeable in undergraduate publications as late as the seventies.

But the last *Burial of Euclid* was in 1860, by the Class of '63, and that by a minority. The class voted fifty-three to thirty-one against it. The thirty-one celebrated, nevertheless, but the ceremony seems to have been tame and perfunctory. The *Lit.* which in 1857 had denounced "the annual disgrace," notices, in the December number of 1860, that the Sophomores had at any rate omitted the tin horns, and is inclined to think the processional part of the old ceremony might well be continued—"its grotesque and goblin disguises, its torches and brilliant fireworks;" only not the tin horns. But the Class of '64 dropped the whole thing silently, without voting. Euclid was never buried again. It had always been Saturnalian, and had grown Bacchanalian. Probably the Faculty discouraged it; the songs imply as much. Possibly the Civil War brought about, among the students themselves, a lapse of gusto for its orgies.

"In its earliest phases, dating far back in the XIX century, the Burial appears to have taken place in the winter or late autumn, and to have had a prefix. In the prefix . . . the volume was perforated with a red hot iron, each man in turn thrusting the iron through the covers—symbolizing the fact that each had 'gone through' Euclid. Then it was held upward and the class paused below, indicating that he was 'understood.' Next each man passed the volume underfoot to prove that Euclid had been 'gone over.' These ceremonials were but preliminary to the Burial, which came later." This prefix was perhaps more nearly the original form of the ceremony.

The ritual varied somewhat with the taste of each class. Sometimes it was the volume, sometimes the effigy of Euclid, that was buried. The programs all mention the grave, but contemporary recollections speak mainly of cremation. Probably he was sometimes both burned and buried. But the following may be taken as a typical description of the ceremony from 1845 to 1860.

On a certain night of the second week in November, at about ten o'clock, the Sophomore class, more or less masqued and costumed, assembled and marched, headed by a band, to a hall known at the time as the "Temple"—now Steinert's Hall, at the corner of Orange and Court Streets. Entry was by password; the "Force Committee" seems to have had charge of admissions; but a large crowd of undergraduates were already gathered there, and on the platform lay the bier and effigy of Euclid. The ceremonials in the hall were normally and in outline something as follows:

1. Music by the band.
2. Song, Latin words to the tune of "Lauriger Horatius" or "Gaudeamus," usually the latter.

3. Music by the band.
4. Oration.
5. Song, to some tune like "Skool, Skool" or "Cocochelunk."
6. Poem.

The orations and poems might seem more scurrilous than witty to an age whose taste for puns is no longer omnivorous. The ceremony in the hall lasted until nearly midnight when the crowd filed out for the procession to the grave, which is the part depicted in the Pageant.

The procession marched with torches and drums and tin horns—especially the horns—by Elm and College to Prospect (then called "Tutor's Lane"), and so to the woods which covered the hillside. The burning or burial took place, according to some traditions, near the present site of the Infirmary.

The familiar lithograph by Davenport, in 1858, as well as recollections of older alumni, prove the Programs to be but the barest skeletons. They prove that the costuming was often elaborate, the revelry varied and extraordinary, and the midnight scene in the woods something which those who are unhelped of recollection can only imagine, and regret that the *Lit.'s* suggestion was not followed, and the burial reformed rather than abolished. The students still sing

> In Sophomore year we have our task,
>   Fol de rol de rol rol rol,
> 'Tis best performed by torch and mask,
>   Fol de rol de rol rol rol—

but what "task" is forgotten.

THE PROCESSION TO THE GRAVE

BANDITTI
(Led by a gorgeous and hilarious drum-major)

THE SOLEMN SINGERS

THE BIER

THE "FORCE COMMITTEE"
(Carrying swords)

FOUR WHOLLY RED DEVILS
(Wheeling four fiery red wheelbarrows)

THE MOURNERS
(Relatives of the deceased)

MADAME EUCLID   PARENT HESIS EUCLID
(His wife)   *(His stepmother)*

AUNTY CEDENT EUCLID
(His aunt)

POLLY GON EUCLID   CORA LEARY EUCLID

ANNA LYTICS EUCLID
(His daughters)

GEO. METRY EUCLID
(His son)

(Upon the garments of Madame Euclid are many triangles whose positive and penetrating acuteness refer to the gossip that the foibles of the deceased were in part due to domestic trials. Aunty Cedent may be known by the circumstance that her head is set on with the face backward. Parent Hesis is a bulbous figure but small waisted. Polly Gon is decorated with regular and irregular designs; Anna Lytics, with X's and Y's in inextricable confusion. Cora Leary is a small child with her hair in a braid behind and herself wholly given to the vicious habit of tagging after. Geo. Metry is a new edition of his progenitor who complacently believes himself to be an improvement. The mourners carry large squares, circles, rhomboids, etc., representing instruments of torture used by the deceased and now hung about the necks of his unpleasant family.)

THE EUCLID HATERS

(*On hobby horses or ponies, symbolical of aids and supports, by which the woes of oppression have been—at times and in some measure—relieved and the tyranny of the oppressor evaded. The horses are spirited, not to say treacherous.*)

THE MATHEMATICAL FACULTY

PROF. PONTIUS I. NORUM
(*Liberally nicknamed the Pilot of Asses, carrying the simulacrum of a well-known, improbable, but ultimately veracious proposition.*)

TUTOR MARCUS LOW
(*One afflicted with underestimation of his fellowmen.*)

IKE AYRE KNOTT ADAM
(*A student lately dropped.*)

A "DIG"   A "DIG"   A "DIG"   A "DIG"
DEVILS   WITCHES   GOBLINS   WIZARDS
INDIANS   CANNIBALS   TURKS
CLOWNS   DUNCES   MONKEYS   SKELETONS
FIREMEN   MINERS   POLICEMEN
FRESHMAN FRESHMAN FRESHMAN FRESHMAN FRESHMAN FRESHMAN
FRESHMAN FRESHMAN FRESHMAN FRESHMAN FRESHMAN FRESHMAN
FRESHMAN FRESHMAN FRESHMAN FRESHMAN FRESHMAN FRESHMAN
FRESHMAN FRESHMAN FRESHMAN FRESHMAN FRESHMAN FRESHMAN
ad lib.

SONGS

Tune, "Gaudeamus"; words by the Class of 1853.

I.

Fundite nunc lacrimas,
Plorate, Yalenses.   } Bis
Euclid rapuerunt fata,
Membra et ejus inhumata
Liquimus tres menses.   Bis

II.

Omnes Praeses expellat, } Bis
Facultas minetur,
Nobis tamen fortiter
Funeri portabitur
Euclid, et condetur.   Bis

Tune, "Old Grimes is Dead"; words by the Classes
of 1853, 1859, 1861.

I.

This night a band of valiant Sophs
With hearts all brave and true,
Have dared the threats of "powers that be"
To render thee their due.
Thy hideous visage, Euclid, now
With sweet delight we burn,
And while we stand together here
Thy minion Tutors spurn.

II.

Black curls the smoke above the pile
And snaps the crackling fire;
The joyful shouts of merry Sophs,
With wails and groans conspire.
May yells more fiendish greet thy ears,
And flames yet hotter glow
May fiercer torments rack thy soul
In Pluto's realms below.

III.

He gave to us such pains, my friends,
       He gave to us such pains,
We justly take some pains for him
       Who gave to us such pains.
Then Farewell Euclid!   Long for thee
       The tear of grief shall fall,
And plaintiff song and l. e. g.
Long, long, thy fame recall.

Tune, "Cocochelunk"; words by the Classes of 1856 and 1859.

I.

Euclid's dead and burnt and buried.   Bear him, Charon, o'er the Styx.
Let him never, hence referried, flunk the Freshman with his tricks.

CHORUS

He is gone and gone forever.   Quaff we deep of Lethe's wave.
All our griefs must be forgotten in our joy of Euclid's grave.

II.

Gone his angles that have bored us; the acute is now obtuse;
Let him angle, with the lines that floored us, in the Stygian stews.

CHORUS—

III.

To the acts of years unnumbered draw we now a parallel.
We are square with Euclid's manes.   Polyphlunking prince, farewell.

CHORUS—

SCENE III

THE KANSAS VOLUNTEERS

By

ROBERT MUNGER

I.

The conflict over slavery was centering in 1856 in control of the territory of Kansas. For two years emigration had continued, north and south attempting to colonize, the south for slavery, the north for freedom. Northern Aid Societies were common in New England, helping with money and equipment those who were eager to settle in Kansas and use all effort that it should be free.

In the early part of 1856, a company of colonists for Kansas had been recruited in New Haven. They went out to new homes with a crusader's spirit in furtherance of a great cause. On March 20, 1856, a benefit meeting for these volunteers was held in North Church, and was addressed by Henry Ward Beecher. Upwards of a thousand dollars was raised for the use of the company. A suggestion was made that the emigrants were unarmed, which precipitated much discussion until finally, upon a proposal favored by Beecher, Professor Silliman of Yale College, and others, pledges were taken to furnish fifty Sharp's rifles. Mr. Dunlap of the Senior Class of Yale College pledged himself to raise twenty-five dollars for a rifle from members of the class. A similar pledge was made by Mr. Moses Tyler, of the Junior Class. The pastor of the church, Reverend Samuel Dutton, presented a Bible and a rifle to Mr. Lines, one of his deacons, who was among the volunteers.

Great feeling was roused by this action taken at the meeting. Various letters were written to the New Haven papers and severe criticism of it was printed in the *Register*. There were various southern members of the Junior Class of the College who were exercised by the report that Tyler had pledged the class for a rifle.

On March 31st, a farewell to the New Haven Kansas Volunteers was held. Sixty members of the company were seated upon the platform. A letter from Beecher was read and the "Kansas Emigrant" song by Whittier was sung to the tune of "Auld Lang Syne," as well as the Western Colonist's song, written to the tune of "God Save the King" for the occasion, by the Reverend Hiram Bingham.

> All hail our glorious west
> Destined to be possessed
> By liberty.
> By compact firm and pure
> While truth and light endure
> From Slavery's blight secure
> Realm of the free.

After the meeting, the company was escorted to the New York boat by citizens, friends in attendance at the meeting, and the New Haven Fire Company.

It was to be only a few weeks afterward, in May, that Sumner was to say in the Senate that the portents of Civil War "hang on all the arches of the horizon." Two days later with the attack on Lawrence, violence and disorder were supreme in Kansas.

CAMP PUTNAM.

The ENCAMPMENT of the NATIONAL GUARD of NEW-YORK, at NEW-HAVEN Conn. June 1852.

To Colonel L.W. Stevens the Officers and Members of the 7 Regiment N.Y.S.A.N.G. This Print is respectfully inscribed, by their obliged servant Orlando Neely Surgeon

II.

Into the West they turn, beyond the flow
Of the broad waters that shall never brim
On one shore bond and on the other free.
Both shall be free! men's eyes were never touched
With clearer vision, looked with larger hope.
East land and West and North and South shall bless
This pilgrimage; God shall take up the prayers
That breathe upon this parting, fold them close
Into His bosom, keep them night and day,
And happier summers blooming in the land
Shall know how they were guided and came home.
A new home now! "free-soil, free speech, free men"
Shall hallow it, make small the cost to those
Who look and find the alien landscape strange.
Field-flower and level harvest of the plain
And river-valley's tillage and nurtured slope
Of dipping hills of Kansas shall come forth
And gather up with them a noble story,
A lengthening honor and a fragrant fame.

Hear now the voice that speaks to those who go
For Freedom's sake to keep the balance fast;
Beecher stands up, his mighty tone sounds forth,
Silliman speaks, "To arm in self-defense
Becomes at such a time a sacred duty."
Dutton, within whose tabernacle rise
The benedictions of the time, speaks out,
Proclaiming arms as holy as the Word
Bestows them, trusting God would have it so.

And she whose son fell first upon the field
That followed fast upon the whirling days
And bleeding cries of Kansas—she is here;
Yale, in whose cherishing halls there rise again
As if with visible form and solemn brow,
The mighty of old time in Liberty,
Pointing the measure of the hour's grim need,
High counsellors of the shades, spirits that speak
With never-dying voices of the past.
"This is the Way, the Time, this shall endure."

Westward! there breathe forever from that name
Strange airs of glory and of far romance,
Escape and new awakenings, proof of heart
And mighty sinew and the dust of things
Cast down and trampled over and put by.
Westward! there is a sound forevermore
Within it of new covenants and cries
Of bitter travail and of faithful days,
Out of it is a tang of ocean blown,
Of sea-spray and lashed foam and barren sands,
There is a vision in it of a land
Piercing the shadows with baptismal brows,
Washed with cool streams of mercy, filled with rest
Under wide skies of peace and kindlier stars
After earth's troubled fevers and vain dreams.
    The severance of this hour may bring alike
For those who go and those who say "Farewell,"
Remembrance of a time gone by, no less
Than Pilgrims of an older day are these
Who fare to a far country, bringing in
Justice of men, Valor and Word of God.

In the Pageant the meeting in North Church and the setting out of the Kansas settlers will be played amid a typical setting of the period, as though the rest of the life of New Haven were passing and repassing across the Green. Families in the somewhat pompous dress of the time meet and discuss the situation. The procession of a girl's school goes by attended by two prim mistresses. Small children are playing at games. Students stroll hither and thither. Ladies in barouches, their faces sheltered from the sun by the tiny parasols of the time, pass each other with cordial but correct recognition.

SCENE IV

THE DEATH OF THEODORE WINTHROP

By

EDWIN OVIATT

> Let me not waste in skirmishes my power,—
> In petty struggles,—rather in the hour
> Of deadly conflict may I nobly die!
> In my first battle perish gloriously!

(From *Waiting,* a poem by Theodore Winthrop of the Yale College Class of 1848, written in 1851.)

Theodore Winthrop wrote these prophetic lines when he was twenty-two years old and beginning a literary career that had much promise of distinction. Ten years later he was to fall,—the first Yale man and, I believe, the first Union officer to be killed in the Civil War,—leading a forlorn hope against a Southern battery at Great Bethal. Poet, novelist, and war correspondent for James Russell Lowell's infant *Atlantic Monthly,* this young Yale graduate gave his life to his country in almost the first battle of the war.

Fort Sumter's guns had just boomed forth the answer of the North to the opening act of the disaffected Southerners. President Lincoln had issued his first ringing call for volunteers to uphold the threatened Union. The whole North was looking toward the Potomac, complacently and with an easy lightness of thought that little anticipated the deluge of blood that was to follow before the question thus raised was to be settled. Regiments were forming and entraining for the brief term of service that everybody was agreed would be sufficient to put down the insurrection. Through the streets of New York, hung with flags and bunting for the occasion, the gallant Seventh gaily marched to stop the uprising in a month's excursion on Virginian soil. A novice at arms, young Winthrop, then but thirty-two years old, dropped his pen and marched off with them as a private soldier, writing to his uncle in the breezy way of these first volunteers, that he was off "to free the slaves." A month later, and he had stayed behind when the Seventh returned, to become the volunteer Military Secretary to General Ben Butler, then commanding the Department of Virginia.

Young Winthrop had said to his mother, as he left their home on Staten Island for the front, "I do not take this step lightly." Throughout his previous literary work there had run a vigorous thread of pent-up nervous force, and his letters from Fortress Monroe, where he was now quartered, show his keen relish for adventure and aggressive action. General Butler having conceived the idea of a sudden attack on some Confederate troops entrenched a few miles away at Bethal, the young Yale aide threw himself with great energy into the plan, and prepared himself to take part in it. Writing to his mother on June 9th, he had said: "We march to-night in two detachments, to endeavor to surround and capture a detachment of the Secession Army, estimated at from three or four hundred to twenty-five hundred. If we find them where we expect, we shall bag some. If I come back safe I will send you my notes of the Plan of Attack. . . . We march at midnight."

These were young Major Theodore Winthrop's last written words. At midnight on the ninth of June, 1861, the two columns of Northern troops left Fortress Monroe for Bethal. The plan of attack was a good one, so military students have always said. Winthrop himself, working with General Butler, had drawn it up, to the smallest details. It was to have been a surprise through two columns simultaneously rushing the Southern battery entrenched across a small stream at Great Bethal. It should have succeeded. Winthrop, ranking as a Major on Butler's staff, had no command himself, but had gone along with the troops to see that the original arrangement was carried out.   That this was not done was no fault of his.   Unprepared, as the North was, to take the field at the unexpected summons to the colors, and manned, as it was, by officers who had little practical knowledge of military tactics, the fiasco of this attack was a typical result of much of the fighting in the early days of war.

For in the darkness of the early June dawn, the careful plans for this attack broke down when two Northern detachments mistook each other and fired, warning the Southerners of their approach.   General Butler's last instructions had been not to attack the Great Bethal battery unless success was certain.   "Be brave as you please," said Butler, "but run no risks."   The order should immediately have been given for retreat, after this opening mistake.   But the inexperienced officers of the Northern columns kept on, through Little Bethal, and to the attack on Great Bethal, where the Southerners were already prepared to meet them.   Matters still might have gone well for the Northern troops had not a second blunder been committed.   In a quick flanking movement to the left, three Northern companies went astray in the bush.   Mistaking them for the enemy their commanding officer thought he himself was being outflanked and retreated.

Expecting the immediate success of this flanking movement, the second column, with Major Winthrop, now started to rush the Confederate battery across the marsh and fields.   A hail of bullets and shot from the field pieces and cannon of the Southerners greeted them and men dropped everywhere.   At this juncture, and when the now completely disorganized commanders were ordering retreat and advance at the same time, Major Winthrop jumped to the front.   Mounting a fallen log, the young Yale aide, who had "all the time been conspicuous at the head of the advancing Federal troops, loudly cheering them on to the assault," was now seen waving his sword and heard calling out above the rifle-and-cannon-fire, "Come on!"

It was at this instant that a Confederate drummer-boy, snatching a rifle from a fellow soldier and leaping to the rebel embankment, shot Winthrop in the chest. The body of the young Yale patriot pitched forward close to the Southern battery, and he was dead.

A week later and that incident occurred, which, while trivial in itself, was as fine an indication as the Civil War gives us of the underlying friendliness between the North and the South. The memory of Theodore Winthrop's heroic death will live long in his country's annals, but the common bond which unites the people will outlive even that. This young Yale graduate's death has done nothing greater for us than to prove the truth of this. For, on June 17, the Confederate troops gave a signal example of their admiration of their enemy's courage and patriotic spirit and brotherly feeling for them. Proceeding, doubtless with a company of Union soldiers, to the Great Bethal battlefield, official messengers from General Butler asked the Southerners for Winthrop's body. The Great Bethal Confederate officers granted the request, and the Union men brought it back to the North for burial.

Lieutenant Butler, of the commanding officer's staff, led this Fortress Monroe party. As it halted on the edge of the Great Bethal fields, he, accompanied by Winthrop's brother in the gray uniform of the New York Seventh and brother-in-law in civilian dress, went under flag of truce to the Southern side and asked for an audience with the Confederate commanding officer. The scene is a striking one. Met at the middle of the battlefield by Colonel Magruder and staff, the Northern party presents General Butler's formal respects and his request for Major Winthrop's body. The request is immediately, and even courteously, granted. Colonel Magruder and staff retire to the Confederate side, and presently return with the body of Winthrop in its pine casket, escorted by three hundred Southern troops. The casket is lowered to the ground by the soldier-bearers, and a salute fired by the troops. The formal thanks of General Butler are tendered to Colonel Magruder by the Northern lieutenant, and the Confederate soldiers march back to their entrenchments. Silently the Northerners return to their side of the field, bringing Winthrop's body with them in a country wagon.   There it is received by the waiting Northern troops, who fire a return salute, and march back with it, to muffled drums, to Fortress Monroe, where it is received with full military honors.

The incident made a great impression on the North at the time, and the newspapers had a good deal to say about it and about the courtesy of the Southern officers.   The latter had said, so the Fortress Monroe newspaper correspondents wrote, that "no truer, braver man ever fell on field of battle."   "Had you had a hundred men as brave as Winthrop," so a Louisiana Colonel at Great Bethal was reported as having said to Lieutenant Butler, "and one to lead when he fell, I should have been a prisoner in Fortress Monroe that night."   There were numerous Northern newspaper editorials on the sacrifice of Winthrop, and more on the act of the Southerners in returning his body.   The Seventh—Winthrop's regiment—met his remains in New York and gave it a military escort across the city to the New Haven train.   In New Haven the city streets had been draped in black, and the military procession which escorted the body to the Grove Street Cemetery (up Chapel Street to College, to Elm, to High, to Grove Street), marched with reversed arms and to a dirge by its band and the tolling of the church bells on the Green.   Professor Noah Porter was in this procession, as were most of the College lads, and Professor Porter pronounced a funeral address at the grave. "When I die," young Winthrop had once asked his mother, "put a granite cross over me."   This had been done, and the first Yale man to fall in the Civil War sleeps his last sleep to-day in the ancient New Haven burying ground, under such a monument.

THIRD INTERLUDE

THE WOODEN SPOON PROM

By

EDWARD BLISS REED

NEW HAVEN JOURNAL AND COURIER, JUNE 20TH, 1856.

"The Promenade Concert of the Junior Class last evening was attended by a very large and brilliant company. The galleries were filled with onlookers while the floor was fully occupied by a gay company of dancers. The youth, beauty, wealth and fashion of our city were present, making the assemblage one of rare grace and elegance."

THE YALE LITERARY MAGAZINE, JULY, 1865.

"On Wednesday evening, June 19th, Helmsmüller's Band, under the auspices of the Spoon Committee, gave the usual Promenade Concert at Music Hall. The attendance was larger than it has been for many years. The hall had been decorated with taste and elegance. The music was bewitching, the ladies divine, 'and all went merry as a marriage bell.'"

> Up two narrow flights I have hastened
>   And here in the gallery row,
> Dejected in spirit and chastened,
>   I gaze on the beauty below.
> With flags for the war that has ended,
>   With bunting and wreaths, Music Hall
> Is a vision entrancing and splendid—
>   I'm alone at the Wooden Spoon Ball.

First the concert; it's hard to live through it,
　All the music they play is a bore.
What soul in the crowd listens to it?
　Not the guests promenading the floor.
I've heard William Tell till I'm weary,
　Donizetti is trash; Meyerbeer
With his Huguenots simply is dreary,
　Were it Lohengrin—hush! She is here.

White hoop-skirt, pink sash at her shoulder,
　Pink rose at her breast, in her hair
With its dark Grecian curls—to behold her
　I lean o'er the railing and stare.
Perhaps it's the heat makes me flighty;
　As I look at her surely I see
Trojan Helen, divine Aphrodite,
　Or the Empress of France, Eugénie.

She moves like a queen through the dancers,
　Like a wave of the sea, never still.
Was ever such grace in the lancers,
　In the redowa, schottische, quadrille?
The last time we met, I remember,
　She was distant and cold as the moon;
She froze me like ice, last December—
　She sees me—she bows,—this is June!

I'm down on the floor in a minute;
　(The best waltz of Helmsmüller's band)
"My dance. We lose time; let's begin it."
　She smiles, and she gives me her hand.
To-morrow she'll beam upon Harry,
　Next week she'll be flirting with Tom,
And it's Jack that she'll probably marry—
　Still we'll dance at the Wooden Spoon Prom.

FOURTH OR MODERN EPISODE

SCENE I

PANELS OF MODERN YALE

By

FREDERICK TREVOR HILL

So many of the notable events in the history of Yale since the Civil War are so fresh to the mind, that to present them in the foreshortened form in which we have treated her earlier history would scarcely be possible. It has therefore seemed wise to set this scene in the form of Panels, as though a sculptor had chiselled out in high relief scenes from Yale history and life during this period, to decorate some cornice of the future.

The following Panels have been chosen as showing the most widely divergent points of view of Yale activity since the Civil War.

PANEL I

1870. In the spring of 1870, Professor Othniel Charles Marsh began his series of explorations in Nebraska, Colorado, Wyoming, Utah, California, and Western Kansas which resulted in the discovery of over a hundred species of extinct vertebrates new to science, including the fossil three and four toed horse, the toothed birds, and the flying dragon or pterodactyl. Professor Marsh's discoveries were accorded the highest praise by Darwin and Huxley and Haeckel, and have probably done more to spread the reputation of Yale in Europe than any other achievement.

The scene represents Marsh working with others at the place in Big Bad Lands, South Dakota, where the fossil bones were discovered; the weather is cold and snow is on the ground. U. S. Cavalry are guarding the explorers and an Indian is showing Marsh a fossil tooth of what he called a "big horse struck by lightning." Marsh was known to the Indians as the "big bone Chief." Some of the Indians were very hostile and this expedition in particular was fraught with much danger to all the scientists.

PANEL II

Banger Day, February 22

1884. For many years prior to 1890, Washington's Birthday was the first occasion when Freshmen were allowed to carry canes. They celebrated the event by parading the town carrying absurdly large canes called "bangers," with which they pounded the flagstones as they marched.

The scene represents a "Banger" parade, the marchers armed with their huge club-like canes and wearing placards on their hats announcing their class numerals.

PANEL III

1896. In June, 1896, the Class of '96 planted, as its class ivy, a cutting from the ivy which grows on the side of the church in Lexington, Va., marking the grave of General Robert E. Lee.

Prior to the Civil War, Yale drew a large percentage of her students from the South, but many years elapsed before she was again well represented in that section of the country. The honor thus paid by the Class of '96 to the distinguished General of the Confederacy, who is slowly but surely coming to be recognized as one of the really great Americans, was highly significant. It demonstrated how completely sectional feeling has died out in this country and emphasized the position of Yale as a national rather than a local university.

The scene represents the planting of the Ivy. Students in cap and gown. The Ivy was planted on the North side of Chittenden Library.

PANEL IV

1898. Shortly after the outbreak of the Spanish War, April, 1898, a number of Yale men formed an organization which at first was known as the Yale Battery and afterwards became Light Battery A, First Connecticut Artillery. It was trained during the summer of 1898 at the Government Post at Niantic, Connecticut, and just prior to the close of the war was assigned to General Wade's Division. It was mustered out of service in September, 1898.

The scene represents a detachment drilling at their guns.

PANEL V

1898. On the last day of April, 1898, the S. S. *Paris* of the American Line was taken over by the Government and converted into a swift auxiliary cruiser or scout known as the *Yale*. Yale University, in recognition of the honor done her, immediately raised a subscription and presented the cruiser with two rapid fire six pounders. The guns were mounted on the forecastle and were christened *Eli* and *Handsome Dan*. A number of Yale graduates served on the cruiser, which took many prizes and did valuable service in holding the Spanish fleet in Santiago. The guns were afterwards presented to the University and are now in the Gymnasium.

The scene represents a crew drilling with one of the guns on the forecastle of the U. S. S. Yale.

PANEL VI

1900.   The Yale Forestry School was established in 1900 through
        the beneficence of Mr. and Mrs. James W. Pinchot, and
their sons, Gifford and Amos R. E. Pinchot.   At the time of its
organization there were only two other institutions on the Western Continent concerned with instruction and research in forestry.
The work of the school has grown steadily and increasingly and
exerts an important influence on the conservation and economic
use of forests in the United States.   At least ten graduates of
this school are now in charge of forest schools established by other
educational institutions since the inauguration of this department at Yale.   Nor is its influence confined to this continent,
for certain of its graduates are engaged in governmental conservation work in Hawaii, the Philippines, South Africa, and
Canada.

*The scene represents a party of students measuring trees at
the summer camp of the school at Milford, Pennsylvania.*

PANEL VII

1904.   In April, 1904, the Yale Foreign Missionary Society
        arrived in Changsha, the capital of Hunan, a central
province of China with a population of twenty millions.   The
first representatives of the Society were the Reverend Brownell
Gage, '98, and his wife, a fully qualified nurse.   From this
beginning there has developed Ya-li in Changsha conducted
partly as a missionary and partly as an educational institution
and hospital.   It cares for over 200 pupils and boasts eight fine
buildings, including a hospital which handles some 2,000 cases
a month.   It is supported entirely by voluntary contributions.
From intense hostility the people have been won to keen interest
in the American college.

*The scene represents the laying of the corner stone of the
hospital in the presence of the Chinese Military Governor, in
1915.*

PANEL VIII

1906.   The custom decreeing that Seniors execute a low bow
to the President as he retires from Chapel is a survival
of an old Puritan church custom.   During the eighteenth century it was quite generally the custom in English churches for
the men of the congregation to bow out the pastor, and thus the
Yale honor to the President originated.

*The scene represents the departure of the President amid the
bowing Seniors.   This is a distinctly Yale custom—not dupli-
cated elsewhere, as far as is known.*

PANEL IX

1911.   In the summer of 1911 the Peruvian Expedition under the
auspices of Yale University arrived at Cuzco, the old
Inca capital of Peru.   The party was in charge of Professor
Hiram Bingham, and the Governments of the United States
and Peru gave their active coöperation.   The expedition contributed much to the knowledge of the scientific world, for it discovered and uncovered an Inca or pre-Inca city called Machu
Picchu containing palaces, temples, baths, and about 150 houses.

*The scene represents the scientists at work uncovering the
buried ruins.   They are escorted by Peruvian government officers dressed in uniform, and assisted by Peruvian Indians dressed
in shawls or blankets, trousers and aprons, yoke shirts and
curiously shaped hats.*

PANEL X

1915.   For many years the day before Commencement at Yale
has witnessed a baseball game between Yale and Harvard,
and it has become the custom to have the class boy throw the first
ball over the plate.

*The scene shows a small boy in reunion costume throwing the
ball to the Yale catcher.   Other players are grouped about watch-
ing the scene.*

PANEL XI

1916. Football as a scientific sport began at Yale in November, 1872, with a game against Columbia. At that time there were fifteen men on each team, the ball was round, and each player wore whatever sort of uniform he fancied.

The scene shows a modern football team in formation with the quarter-back preparing to throw the ball.

PANEL XII

1916. On Sunday, June 20, 1915, there was unveiled in Memorial Hall the Yale Civil War Memorial. It contains the names of 113 Yale men who fell on the Union side and 55 who fell on the Confederate side. No names are included save of those who died prior to January 1, 1866.

Wm. W. Gordon, '86 S., son of General Gordon of Savannah, Ga., made the address, Judge Simeon E. Baldwin presented the memorial to the University, and President Hadley accepted it.

The scene represents the unveiling of the tablet, curtained by American flags. Students appear in cap and gown with one or two U. S. Army and Confederate uniforms showing. The tableau represents the instant of the speaking of the lines,

Love and tears for the Blue,
Tears and love for the Gray.

PANEL XIII

1916. The Yale fence is the social center of democracy in the College. There all the Academic Classes gather for talk and song, and it is there that all that is important in the undergraduate world is discussed and settled.

The scene represents a gathering at the fence, some of the men in baseball togs, some in tennis flannels, and others in ordinary street costume; a newspaper boy, in the foreground, offering papers; an elm tree, in the background, showing poster of a Yale-Harvard game.

PANEL XIV

1916. Success in rowing in the annual regattas between Yale
and Harvard has been equally divided between the two
Universities. Each has won twenty-five of the fifty races held
thus far.

*The scene represents the Yale crew carrying the shell on their
shoulders preparatory to launching it. Near by stand the coach
and the coxswain with his megaphone.*

ODE

IN COMMEMORATION OF THE YALE VETERANS OF THE SPANISH–AMERICAN WAR

By

L. FRANK TOOKER

In France the poppies bloom on many a plain
   The blood of Europe's noblest youth has fed.
There lie potential statesmen, poets slain
   In their first promise, saints untimely dead,
   And those who thought to wed
All life to beauty.   Surely now we hear
   A voice o'er Eden calling, "Why? Why? Why?"
   Only the leering Fates can make reply.
Above the darkling world they lean and jeer,
   "Is it not, then, enough to make a shade
   Where lizards drowse at noon and hares run unafraid?"

Tall Troy and Babylon lie low in dust,
   Their warfare over, battles lost and won;
Great Charles's armor has dissolved to rust.
   Where are the bounds he set?   The rolling sun
   Sees all he did undone.
Such age-long strife among the sons of men!
   So many wars, so little righted wrong!
   So much mad storming at one gate to throng
Back through the same gate but to turn again!
   Oh, mad futility!   What gain can light
   With glow-worm lantern such immensity of night!

And yet the light is there.   Was ever ill
  So great it had no compensating gain?
See France regenerate!   See Belgium thrill
  With new-born loyalty!   No loss or pain
  Can make those high ends vain.
Mysterious woes that make the hideous fair!
  Strange passions that ennoble and set free!
  To-day, through France, go men who cannot see
Who, questioned, smile and answer, *"C'est la guerre."*
  No more—that's war, where body is but clay,
  But soul, unconquered, holds its high, untroubled way.

And Cuba freed!   In that amazing war
  How rose our nation to the loud appeal!
Lovers of peace, we chose what we abhor;
  Unhating, gloated when we saw Spain reel
  Before our walls of steel.
Consummate idealists, scorning gain or fee,
  Gay and imperturbable seekers for a sign,
  We romped into our casual battle-line
Merely to set an alien people free,
  Deaf to a doubting world's opprobrious flings,
  Lords of the potency of immaterial things.

And Yale men heard the call, and quickly passed
  Along the road that bridges death and life.
All—all they gave, nor reckoned first or last
  What price would be exacted for the strife.
  For some the road was rife
With petty ills that drag the body down
  While spirit, strong-winged still, strains for the goal;
  In pestilential camps some paid Death's toll;
And some, in leash, gained neither cross nor crown.
  Theirs was in truth the harder lot—to know
  The spurs that urge to battle, yet never face a foe.

Yet faced far more: control and discipline
    Wherein one learns there is no last or first;
The strength to stand and wait while others win;
    The vision to perceive best may be worst
    When men for glory thirst.
Life goes not back.   What yesterday they won
    Walks with to-day.   For those who conquer, woe
    Comes as the wind comes, as the shadows go,
A moment loud or dark, then calm or sun.
    And grim to-morrow—it, like yesterday,
    Shall greet the eyes of those whom nothing can dismay.

Bring myrtle and bring rue and laurel green
    To deck the graves where our dead soldiers lie.
Through that veil that divides unseen from seen,
    With inward-turning vision, we descry
    Them slowly trooping by.
Beside the noble pageant we unroll,
    Here with their comrades—here they mutely pass
    With silent feet across the unbending grass.
Forever young, still seeking their far goal,
    They fare across the pageant of the mind
    High avatars of dreams that consecrate mankind.

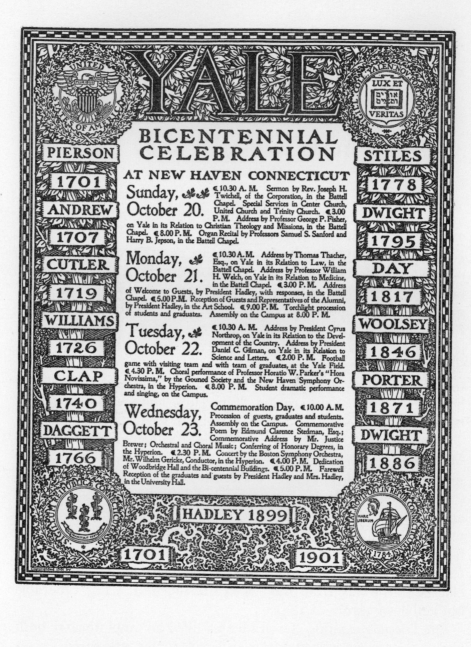

THE YALE BICENTENNIAL

By

HENRY SEIDEL CANBY

The Bicentennial of the founding of Yale at Saybrook in 1701, was celebrated at New Haven on the finest days of October, the 20th to the 24th, in 1901. It was in many respects the most picturesque, most enthusiastic, and most impressive function ever held in an American university. Over nine thousand Yale men, graduates and undergraduates, took part, three hundred and thirty-one delegates represented other collegiate institutions and learned societies, American, European, and Asiatic, and more than sixty honorary degrees were conferred upon the most distinguished group of men that an American university has ever honored. Upon that occasion, John Hay, Horace Howard Furness, John La Farge, Archbishop Ireland, Charles Eliot Norton, Thomas Bailey Aldrich, Mark Twain, William Dean Howells, Marquis Ito, Theodore Roosevelt, and Woodrow Wilson were welcomed as members of the fraternity of Yale.

Five thousand Yale men, costumed to represent the historic ages of the University, marched on Monday night from the campus aglow with orange lanterns, and set about with great bowls blazing with burning rosin, through the streets of New Haven. Carrying torches and colored fire, the long line bore with it classes all the way from 1905, then Freshmen, to a few venerable but active survivors of 1844.

On Tuesday evening the graduates filled an amphitheatre built about a stage upon which the undergraduates presented scenes from the history of Yale. This was the first open air presentation of historical scenes under modern conditions, and may earn for Yale the name of "Mother of Pageants." Classes were grouped together, and in the waits between the scenes each introduced its favorite old-time songs.   It was then that—

> Show me the true-hearted son of old Eli
> Who doesn't love the spot (*three slaps on the left breast*)
> Where the elm tree grows—

was restored to prodigious and lasting favor, and "It was my last Cigar" made a triumphant re-entry into popularity.   At the end of the evening, the audience of nine thousand stood bareheaded singing the Doxology, as at the end of Chapel service, while bombs burst overhead and stars of fire rained through the elm tops,—thus, so said an observer afterward, "praising God and raising hell," in good Yale fashion.

The more formal aspects of the Bicentennial were worthy of its high significance.   To the testimony which the various ceremonies bore to the long service and the lasting responsibility of Yale may be traced much of the confidence, the earnestness, and the enthusiasm of the decade and a half that has succeeded.   A group of distinguished graduates in memorable addresses presented the great evidences of Yale's contribution to law, to medicine, to religion, to legislation, to letters, to philology, to science and education generally, and to every department of our civilization.   A Greek ode, by Professor Goodell, the fine commemorative poem, "Mater Coronata," read by the author, Edmund Clarence Stedman, the singing of Professor Parker's "Hora Novissima," a concert by the Boston Symphony Orchestra, were part of a program that continued without cessation for four days.   Not least in memory was the reappearance from honored retirement of a Yale man of letters of another generation, Donald G. Mitchell ("Ike Marvel") of the Class of 1841, to present his last contribution to American literature in honor of the dedication of Woodbridge Hall.   His rich and graceful history of the American family for whom the hall was named was a blessing from the older time upon the third century of Yale.

Deeply impressive was the academic procession, with two Presidents of the United States, one *de facto,* one prospective, in its ranks, a Secretary of State, a Justice of the Supreme Court, a Premier of Japan, college presidents from nearly all important American institutions, and distinguished scientists, scholars, writers, preachers, and legislators from all over the world. Within the Hyperion theatre, towards which it moved (Woolsey Hall was not yet completed), admission for the generality was unattainable, and many a recent graduate was present at the crowning ceremonies of the Bicentennial only because he remembered the hidden way by which in undergraduate days he had been admitted to the company of the "supes."

It was upon this occasion of commemoration and the conferring of degrees that President Hadley achieved a reputation for epigrammatic characterization of eminent service which has been sustained at many Commencements since. "On you," he said to Professor Woodrow Wilson, "who, like Blackstone, have made the studies of the jurist the pleasure of the gentleman, and have clothed political investigations in the form of true literature, we confer the degree of Doctor of Laws"; and of President Roosevelt: "He is a Harvard man by nurture; but in his democratic spirit, his breadth of national feeling, and his earnest pursuit of what is true and right, he possesses those qualities which represent the distinctive ideals of Yale, and make us more than ever proud to enroll him among our alumni"; to which the President replied, "I have never yet worked at a task worth doing that I did not find myself working shoulder to shoulder with some son of Yale." This gathering of the leaders of American life and thought with representatives of the best of Europe, assembled to do honor to Yale and be honored by her, was the close and chief celebration of the Bicentennial.

The great service of the Bicentennial to Yale, however, was not the mere assemblage of national leaders in New Haven, nor its function as a reunion of college classes on an unprecedented scale, nor the dignified Bicentennial group of buildings then dedicated as a lasting monument, nor even the splendid impulse towards development along true university lines thus given to Yale and renewed continuously since. It was rather the realization of the historic past of Yale and her accumulated dignities, the opportunities and the responsibilities thereof, which then came first with emphasis to the college generations in whose hands the future of the university was to rest. Beneath the excitement of that Bicentennial week, and beyond its pomp and ceremony, was the consciousness of an institution that was more than stone and mortar, more than endowment, more even than men; a trust of inestimable dignity, a heritage of ideals, and a name commanding veneration as well as love. Much of what Yale seemed to demand of that generation has been realized; much more remains to be achieved. But the sense of historic continuity once aroused is powerful upon the future. It tempers pride by responsibility; it makes loyalty self-confident, yet modest because aware of the high examples of the past. Yale has been less provincial, less tamely conservative, more earnest, and more mindful that lasting tenure comes from enduring service to the state, since the great awakening of the Bicentennial.

The scene represented in the Pageant of 1916 is the academic procession of the faculty, honored guests, and distinguished representatives, as with the President of the United States at the head, it moved from the campus through the archway of Vanderbilt to the Hyperion for the ceremonies of commemoration and the granting of degrees.

SCENE III

THE YALE BATTERY

By

ROBERT MELVILLE DANFORD

(Major, U. S. A.; Colonel, Connecticut National Guard)

During the past year educators throughout the United States have become seriously impressed with the need of a more general and a more accurate understanding of the military problems of our country. They have been impressed with our utter impotence as a military power, and they have become startled with the conviction that our American lads are reaching manhood "more accustomed to the enjoyment of privileges than to the fulfilment of duties under our government." There is a sentiment crystallizing amongst them that every young man owes service to his country, and that it is "honorable and praiseworthy to render such service." Happily enough these impressions are not confined to the older heads in our colleges and universities, but are enthusiastically and patriotically indorsed by students and undergraduates.

With the example of England before them to-day college men are beginning to realize the truth of the statement made in the United States Senate in 1862 by the Hon. Mr. Sergeant that "the practical operation of the volunteer system has been that the earnest lovers of the country among the people, the haters of the rebellion, the noblest and best of our citizens, have left their homes to engage in this war to sustain the Constitution, while the enemies of civil liberty, those who hate the Government and desire its failure in this struggle, have stayed at home to embarrass it by discontent and clamor. By this system we have had the loyal States drained of those who could be relied upon in all political contests to sustain the Government; going forth to fight the manly foe in front, the covert foe left behind has opened fire in the rear."

It is college men in time of peace who lead the thoughts and shape the convictions of our people, and it is college men in time of war who are the first to sacrifice themselves and who must lead our troops in their battles. Faculties and students are beginning to feel the duties and responsibilities of this leadership, and all over the country they are now engaged in awakening, in the most practical sort of way—that by example—the conviction that the national defense of all institutions, should be the most democratic, that it is one where a common, a universal sacrifice, is needed, not merely a sacrifice of the few in whom the sense of duty is the most keen, the most self-sacrificing, and the most patriotic.

It should be a matter of profound satisfaction to all Yale men that this great university has taken the lead in this movement for a broader, a more unselfish, and a more practical interpretation of one of the greatest duties of citizenship. Inspired by the outspoken, fearless, and patriotic stand of their University President, Yale undergraduates in October, 1915, organized for military instruction and training, to be introduced in the University as an extra-curriculum activity. Upon the advice of Major General Wood, Yale devoted its attention to strengthening one of the weakest points in our military line—the field artillery—which possesses less than 30% of the ammunition and guns, and less than 11% of the trained officers and men needed by an army of 450,000 men. The War Department made it plain that Yale's efforts in this direction were profoundly appreciated, and that every assistance possible under the existing laws would be rendered.

The Yale Battalion consists of four batteries organized on November 22nd, 1915, as a part of the National Guard of Connecticut. Although these batteries aggregate over 480 men, nearly 500 other undergraduates had to be refused enrollment because the quota allowed by law was filled. The undergraduate field artilleryman at Yale is marked by the earnest and sober manner in which he has set about the task of learning the technique of modern field artillery. He has discovered that an officer of field artillery cannot be trained through the study of manuals, regulations, and map problems alone, but that he must have actual and practical knowledge of how guns are laid, how they are maneuvered, and how they are fought. It is the plan to have the military instruction at Yale conducted in such a thoroughly practical way as to qualify a large percentage of the undergraduate field artillerymen as dependable officers of this important arm should war render their services necessary or desirable.

What the War Department has given to Yale in the matter of guns, field artillery equipment and horses, is measurable in dollars and cents, but what Yale can and will give to the Nation in return is without price.

A battery of field artillery in the United States Service includes 4 guns, 12 caissons, and 2 wagons for supplies and spare parts. The "firing battery" includes the 4 guns and 6 of the caissons. The remaining carriages form the "combat train" and do not appear on the firing line.

Two firing batteries, complete except for horses, will appear in the Bowl, entering simultaneously one from the south, the other from the north, side. Each will be preceded by its respective battery commander, who will be accompanied by his detail. These men constitute the element of the organization that controls and directs the battery when operating as a fighting unit.

On entering the Bowl, each battery will turn to the left, will form in double section column, and will move to the end of the Bowl, where it will suddenly be stripped and made ready for fighting by the command, "Action Right!" The battery commander, from a simulated hillock supposed to be hiding the exact location of his battery, will set up his fire control instruments and by means of his signallers will conduct the fire of his battery.

FINALE

YALE, THE MOTHER OF COLLEGES AND MEN

By

T. LAWRASON RIGGS

To strains of solemn music, thirty figures, robed in festal pomp, come slowly into the Bowl, and passing solemnly across it, proceed to the steps leading to the aisles, up which they pass and take their stations before the thirty portals. They are the Daughters of Yale, the Universities and Colleges whose first Presidents were Yale graduates, or in whose development Yale men have exerted a potent and essential influence. The Daughters salute one another, indicating by their gestures that all are come for the loyal greeting of their Mother on her day of jubilee. Lux, the Spirit of Light, appears, and voices her message.

Lux.

Light am I!
From on high
A living lamp I came,
To kindle the altar of Mother Yale,
Her sacred hearth, her beacon bright,
To all her sons a world-revealing flame;
Whereby they strive to pierce through Nature's veil,
The lore of eld to read aright,
And scan the paths the wise have trod,
The paths that lead to God!

The Daughters.

> Hail to thee, Light!
> God saw that thou wert good
> On the primal day.
> Shine on our Mother's queenly way,
> Shine on our spirit-banded sisterhood.
> Hail to thee, Light!

(Veritas, the Spirit of Truth, appears, and voices her message.)

Veritas.

> Truth am I!
> Unborn and ne'er to die,
> Changeless, awful guide to Man!
> Whom Mother Yale,
> Since her glad day began,
> Hath taught her sons to serve,
> With hearts that being humble, shall not fail,
> With eyes that shall not,
> Seeking, by their Mother's grace,
> Some quickening vision of my face,
> Hearing from star and sod,
> My voice that tells of God.

The Daughters.

> Hail to thee, Truth!
> Like God, thou art hid
> From presumptuous eyes.
> And light that seeks thee not, in darkness dies.
> Our sons in turn to worship thee we bid.
> Hail to thee, Truth!

Lux and Veritas.

> All hail, ye daughters pure and strong,
> Daughters all glorious, hail!
> Vestals and pilgrims of Light and Truth,

Bringers of both to the hearts of youth,
Hail, that in splendor throng
Once more to greet your Mother Yale!
Lo, from the central flame,
Torches ye carried forth
To light the East and North
In the great Mother's name!
Lo, at her high behest,
Ye bear the holy fire,
Fervent with brave desire
To light the South and West!
Throughout the land ye went,
Bearing new light
That left the old more bright,
Showing old truth anew
To man's increasing view,
That Light and Truth may everywhere be blent!
Hail, daughters pure and strong,
Vestal and pilgrim throng!

(Now Mother Yale appears upon a stately chariot, which halts in the center of the Bowl. Nine Chief Ministers accompany the Mother, who are the Departments of the University, and these nine do homage to her one by one.)

The College

My scope transcends the bourns of age and race,
I show thy sons whatever Man has done;
That, going forth, a thousand tasks to face,
Their souls in eager service may be one!

The Sheffield Scientific School

The marvel of unfolding Life I tell,
The ordered courses of the stars I scan;
Old darkness shall my missioners dispel,
And harness lightning to the will of Man.

The Graduate School

Patient, within thy temple's grove I bide,
Where the loud traffic of the world is stilled,
And chosen sons, who take my lore for guide,
A never-finished shrine of knowledge build.

The Law School

I voice the garnered verdicts of the just,
The rights of men and nations I define;
Who earn my charter, bear a sacred trust
To show how Freedom's cause is linked to mine.

The School of Religion

Lest eyes be blinded by the lights of earth,
To gather grapes of thorns lest ye be fain,
Remember still the soul's eternal worth—
Know God, or all your knowledge is in vain!

The Medical School

My knights shall ponder nature's healing laws,
Till I my hard-gained accolade bestow;
Their swords I consecrate to Mercy's cause,
And forth to truceless war with Pain they go.

The Music School

Spirit shall speak to spirit, through mine art,
High eloquence that conquereth the years.
I free from shackling toils the harassed heart
And tune it to the choirings of the spheres.

The School of the Fine Arts

In Beauty's name I bid the land rejoice,
Her sacred wine for thirsting souls I pour;
Working responsive to her golden voice,
My sons shall add fresh vintage to her store.

The Forest School

An ancient craft with science new I teach,
The hills' God-woven vesture is my care,
Hemlock and oak, maple and pine and beech,
Waste not—or mourn a ravished land and bare!

(The sound of a great multitude rejoicing is heard, and all the persons who have shown forth the History of Yale pour into the Bowl, while leading the van are the figures of the original towns of Connecticut.)

The Mother.

Welcome, ye loyal daughters, met to grace
With crowning majesty this festal place!
Shall not my heart with holiest joy be fraught,
Marking what growth the fertile years have brought?
A seed was planted, and its tender shoot,
Borne to a neighboring soil, again took root;
Wise toilers tended it, and passed to peace,
For lo! God blessed the tree with rich increase
Till now, when twice a hundred years are sped,
In giant compass are its branches spread,
Where eager throngs for ninefold knowledge seek,
Hearing my ministers their message speak.
But ye, my daughters, are my chiefest pride,
In you are all my powers multiplied.
O blessing past expectance, thus to know
That by your might my heritage shall grow!
For now, as never, need our souls be strong,
Since grappled nations still their strife prolong;
Now Faith is shook, and Knowledge laughed to scorn,
While brothers' hearts by brothers' hands are torn.
Then let our kindred voices loud proclaim
Unchanging hope no changing years can shame,
Declare we, through the nations' breadth and length
Our fathers' faith, whose vision wrought our strength:
That Godwards still, with Light to guide his eyes,
And Truth to rule his heart, mankind shall rise!

(When the Mother has spoken, the whole multitude kneel, and the spectators join them in a hymn for the blessing of God, sung to the old tune, Adeste Fideles, while the Daughters pass forth to fulfill their world mission.)

Lord God Almighty!
Who hast blessed our fathers,
Bless us and guide us by
     Thy Holy Light!
Help Thou our striving
Towards Thy Truth Eternal!
   To Thee be the glory,
   To Thee be the glory,
   To Thee be the glory,
For evermore!
       AMEN!

THE END OF THE PAGEANT.

By G. H. Langzettel

TRUMBULL ART GALLERY—LATER "THE TREASURY"

ESSAYS ON YALE

TWENTIETH CENTURY YALE

By

ARTHUR TWINING HADLEY

Fifty years ago there were few institutions in the United States that could rightfully claim the title of university, either on account of the standards of their scholarship, the character of their instruction, or the reputation of their individual professors. To-day there are many. New endowments, like those of Cornell or Chicago, vie in munificence with those of Harvard or Yale. State universities are supported by the public on a scale which provides for a still larger annual expenditure than that of privately endowed institutions. Under these circumstances some people have predicted that universities like Yale would lose their importance; that those who wished their education to be cheap or practical or progressive would resort to new places and leave the old ones wrapped up in a mantle of traditionalism.

This prophecy has not been fulfilled. The new have not crowded out the old. There has been a differentiation of work between new and old which enables each class of institutions to render the kind of service for which it is specially fitted.

President Harper once said that the thing which Yale had and which Chicago did not and could not have was Connecticut Hall. The things for which it stands cannot be bought for money or created in a day. "A university is not a school but an atmosphere." The Yale atmosphere has distinctive qualities arising out of the long history behind us; and it is precisely these qualities which enable Yale and places like Yale to render distinctive services to their students and to the country.   They have a body of traditions which are valuable in themselves and doubly valuable under existing circumstances in American life.   They are places where for generation after generation men have been giving devoted service to the teaching of letters and of science.   The example of unselfishness and idealism set by these men has meant more than their concrete teaching itself.   They have transmitted to their students a respect and an enthusiasm for the kind of things they themselves were doing.   They have trained up graduates loyal to these ideals at a time when such ideals and such loyalty are greatly needed in the affairs of the nation and the world.

Yale stands to-day more distinctively than ever before on the side of idealism against commercialism.   Both in his college course and in his professional school life, the boy is influenced to make capacity for service the goal of his ambition rather than capacity to make money.   Our college has been a place where men were trained for public service.   Our technical schools have been nurseries of professional progress even more than of professional success.

Yale also stands on the side of continuity against the restless pursuit of novelty.   We are accused of being unprogressive.   We can face the accusation calmly when we remember that Yale originated the American system of graduate instruction and the American system of agricultural education; that she had the first university school of the fine arts, and that she has to-day the leading university press of the country.   People do not always recognize how important these things are, because they have grown out of small beginnings.   But their success and the success of other things like them emphasizes the fact that true progress represents quiet and continuous movement rather than a series of spectacular jumps.

Finally, Yale stands for poetry as distinct from prose.   It is hard to define just what this statement means; but every Yale graduate who looks back on the years of his college life will see that the things whose remembrance he most cherishes are not those that he could most easily justify by utilitarian standards; that he loves Yale because she is a place that has grown, instead of being made to order; that the word Alma Mater is no unmeaning metaphor, but represents a permanent object of loyalty and of affection which are delightful in their very irrationality.

These are things for which Yale stands, and these are things which the country needs. Those who complain that Yale is unpractical or irrational or prefers history to headlines are simply emphasizing their own need for the distinctive kind of service that Yale renders. As long as the country is over full of men who are pursuing temporary forms of success, or fads in literature and art and politics, or the immediate conventional objects which can be expressed in prose instead of the more subtle and elusive ideals which constitute the poetry of life, lessons like those given by Yale to-day will continue to be needed. No man can tell what changes in organization the next century will witness. No one can predict the alterations in methods of teaching and in subjects taught. But the Yale ideals and standards of to-day are so distinctive, so necessary to the American people, and so deep rooted in the hearts of Yale graduates, that they are likely to inspire Yale's whole contribution to twentieth century civilization.

YALE'S CONTRIBUTION
TO THE SPANISH-AMERICAN WAR

By

WILLIAM HOWARD TAFT

History is again repeating itself, and, therefore, in order to understand the patriotic and martial spirit which suddenly animated Yale University in 1898, we have only to transplant into that period the wave of enthusiasm and devotion which has just swept over us. Not only in spirit, but even in detail, does the parallel hold. Those of us who remember that sultry spring night, two years ago, when, at the first sign of serious trouble in Mexico, fifteen hundred students suddenly began to parade around the Yale Campus, cheering the flag and the country, will not be surprised to learn that on the same kind of night, in the spring of 1898, there occurred a demonstration of almost the same sort. In fact, the two demonstrations were alike even to the details of calling upon President Hadley, then Professor Hadley, and Professor Phelps, for speeches upon the merits of a war. There were several popular demonstrations during the months just preceding the war, one of which the *Alumni Weekly* described as follows:

On Monday afternoon [March 28, 1898] a few Sophomores began parading on the Campus in front of Farnam Hall. Their cheers for "Cuba Libre" soon attracted more of their classmates, and the company, now augmented till it numbered about thirty, marched to Pierson Hall, where a large number of Sophomores room. Here about thirty more recruits were enrolled. From Pierson the company marched to the Hutchinson on Crown Street, where still more Sophomores joined the parade.

In front of the Hutchinson the recruits were divided into companies, while every man who was able to secure a sword appointed himself an officer. The adjutant reported, after inspecting arms, that the company was provided with one musket, two brooms, two flags, and various swords and sabres. These arms were relics, for the most part, of the Civil War.

From the Hutchinson the Sophomores, under the command of Provisional Colonel Julian Day, proceeded to the Green, where they marched, countermarched, and charged imaginary regiments of Spaniards, to the considerable interest of the crowd which had gathered to watch them. After this drill the company marched through Phelps Gateway, gave a cheer for Cuba Libre, and disbanded.

These demonstrations, however, were not merely a sign of spring and full spirit. Directly after, the weekly military drill, which was then a regular but optional course at Yale, began to be attended by an increasing number of men, and a little while later, on April 25th, it was announced that a Yale Battery, consisting of 175 men, would be organized and prepared for action. Great enthusiasm greeted this announcement and in a very short time the required number of men had enlisted and were ready to begin training. The men were sent to Niantic, Connecticut, after some delay in securing their equipment, and began active preparation for war. The Yale men who were appointed as officers of the Battery were: H. T. Weston, '98 S., 2d lieutenant; D. C. Twitchell, '98, and F. V. Chappell, '98 S., sergeants.

On the day after the departure of the Yale Battery for Niantic, we find the following tribute in the *Journal and Courier:*

The real "Yale spirit" stuck right out yesterday morning when the Yale volunteers for the light battery answered the roll-call in the armory and left the city to go into camp at Niantic. There are those in the colleges and out who are thinking and saying that fine young men who are being educated can "do better" than to go to War, and they cheerfully imply that it is well enough to let other young men who are not so fine and not so educated do the hard work of fighting for the country. The Yale volunteers do not agree with such thinkers and sayers. Their patriotic impulse has swept away all selfish thought of their "bright prospects" and their "opportunities." They have forgotten that if they should stay at home and attend to business they might, by proper maneuvering, become congressmen, senators, bishops, professors, judges and other big things. They have thrown trimming prudence to the winds and have declared by their action their overwhelming love for their country and their willingness to freely give all they have and all they are for it. Foolish boys, say some of the calm thinkers who are coolly and cautiously trying to balance themselves and things in these unusual and exciting times. Noble boys, say those who are still capable of being thrilled by unselfish patriotism and who do not value matter above spirit. God's blessing on the Yale volunteers. They are fine young men indeed, and they are right in line with the highest spirit and the grandest record of their nourishing mother.

One of the never-to-be forgotten events of this period was the great patriotic meeting held in College Street Hall on Friday night, May 20, 1898, when feeling rose to an unprecedented pitch and when hearts beat high with a reawakened love of country. The speakers of the evening were President Timothy Dwight, Dr. E. S. Lines, and Professor Bernadotte Perrin. Several members of the Yale Battery were in town at the time, and their appearance in uniform at the meeting provoked a storm of applause. All of the speeches were of a stirring character; but the following lines from the speech of Dr. Lines may be taken as representative of the entire assembly: Dr. Lines said, among other things:

We send to-night from the old home to the great family of the sons of Yale, the assurance that the new men in our long muster-roll appreciate the need of the new time. Yale men are giving themselves for the country's service even as Yale men did in the war for Independence and in the Civil War, and are thoughtful and sober-minded. It is hopeful to see the college community stirred by the sense of responsibility to the country and brought to feel that sacrifices must be made for the State. A new generation of College men is learning how much the country means for them and that patriotism is more than zeal for party, fervid oratory, and display of flags.   The war has touched the heart of the University and the response is worthy of her best traditions.

One of the indelible events of this period was the decision of the United States Government at Washington to give to the well-known liner "Paris," which was being transformed into an auxiliary cruiser, the name of "Yale."   This act on the part of Washington touched the heart of every Yale man to the very core; for it was a most striking recognition, on the part of the Government, of the regard and esteem in which Yale was held by the country.   Nor was the satisfaction over this fact lessened by the fact that another boat was named the "Harvard."   It only added fuel to the fire of college enthusiasm, for it brought home the consciousness that, in the greatest of all struggles, Yale and Harvard were not rivals but partners.

The concrete substance of Yale's appreciation of the honor which had been shown her by the country was at once forthcoming.   By means of a popular subscription, a sum of money was quickly raised with which to buy a brace of guns and a set of colors for the "Yale."   The guns were placed on board with due ceremony and formed an important and useful part of the Yale's equipment.   It may come as a surprise to many to learn that the two guns which they have so often seen in the Trophy Hall of the Yale Gymnasium, and which may be seen there to this day, are "Handsome Dan" and "Eli," the guns that were given by Yale to her namesake and which were returned at the expiration of their term of usefulness.

It is impossible to recount here, in detail, the names and the histories of all those who served their country in the Spanish-American War.   However, during the short period of the war, 300 Yale men enlisted in the Army and Navy at the President's call for volunteers.   Of this number, 215 were graduates and 85 were undergraduates.   A remarkably large proportion of this number, over 25 per cent, or 96 in number, were commissioned officers.   Out of this number there were two Brigadier-Generals, 3 Colonels, 5 Lieutenant-Colonels, 10 Majors, 21 Captains, and 55 Lieutenants.

Five men died in the service of their country.   The roll of honor is:

Rodmond Vernon Beach, '87,
Loten Abijah Dinsmoor, *ex-*'94,
Lazarus Denison Stearns, '96 S.,
Gerard Merrick Ives, '96,
Theodore Westwood Miller, '97.

The truth is that the college period of life is the one in which pure ideals are most easily roused and the flame of patriotism evoked by danger to the country burns as intensely among college men as anywhere in the country.   Their sense of obligation to sacrifice themselves is real.   They then weigh less the cost than later on in life.   So it has been in all our wars.   So it is to-day in the enthusiasm with which the Yale Battery has been formed, and the eagerness and thoroughness shown in the drill and discipline of a difficult branch of the military art.   The closing line in the great Yale song, "Bright College Days," is not a mere poetic sentiment, but expresses the profound feeling of the Yale Student body: "For God, For Country, and For Yale."

YALE AND NEW HAVEN IN 1716

By

ELISABETH WOODBRIDGE MORRIS

Two hundred years ago the Connecticut lad who was bent upon gaining a collegiate education was met by a rather odd difficulty: the difficulty of deciding where his college really was. A college, or, as it was more modestly called, a "collegiate school," had indeed been recently established at Saybrook, but in the year 1716 its trustees, after years of wrangling, voted to remove it to New Haven. This vote, however,—hotly contested by a strong faction favoring Hartford,—seemed at the moment to have decided nothing. Its immediate effect was rather to let loose the centrifugal forces always present in a human institution. The Collegiate School became, not one, but three. Thirteen students did, it is true, assemble at New Haven, but fourteen were collected at Wethersfield, through the industry or at least with the encouragement of Timothy Woodbridge and the other Hartford-minded trustees. Here, under a particularly interesting tutor, Elisha Williams, they pursued their collegiate course, and in September of this very year 1716, on the same day that the New Haven students were celebrating their Commencement, the Wethersfield students celebrated theirs. While at New Haven four young scholars were receiving their degrees, one, up at Wethersfield, was receiving his at the hands of the recalcitrant trustee, Timothy Woodbridge. To complete the confusion, a remnant of the school, three or four students, stayed on at Saybrook, where the library also remained.

Where, then, really was the college? The Connecticut scholar-lads answered the question variously. Jonathan Edwards, in this very year of 1716, at the ripe age of thirteen, enrolled himself as a student at Wethersfield, and not until Senior year did he, with the rest of the Wethersfield group, permanently remove to New Haven. Other Connecticut lads, however, resisted the allurements of Wethersfield with its brilliant tutor, and of Saybrook with its imposing, if unused, library. Coming to New Haven, in the fall of 1716, what did they find here?

They probably came on horseback, bringing with them their few books. Probably, too, they followed the "Pequot Trail," by that time the well-established post road between Boston and New York. And whether they approached from the East or from the West, they must, as they neared their journey's end, have come out upon much the same great stretches of green and tawny salt marsh that we see to-day, with cultivated fields farther inland, northward of the town, and the little square town itself set diamond-wise at the inner curve of the long harbor, its original outline still emphasized by the old palisade that surrounded it. As they entered by some gate near the east or the west angle (now the corner of George and York, or State and Grove) the inner plan or pattern of the town—eight squares about a central square—must have been similarly emphasized to the eye by the board fences that surrounded each square. Looking across these fences the boys could see the scattered farmhouses with their flower and vegetable gardens and their bits of pasturage.

Between these lines of solid fencing the streets ran straight and level, but still thick-fringed with weeds and bushes, and beset with ditches, rocks, and stumps. At the market-place, which was not fenced, they could look across to the other side of the little town, for the square had been cleared of trees, though not of stumps, weeds, or geese. Near its center stood the little square hip-roofed meeting-house. On its College Street side was the little house which then lodged the Hopkins Grammar School, a slightly larger jail beside it, with pillory, stocks, and whipping post, and just beyond them the "county-house" and watch house.

Near the west corner of the market place, our newly arrived scholars perhaps drew up before "Miles Tavern" (about where the "Taft" stands to-day), and asked to be directed to the new college. Probably they were sent on to the house of the Reverend Mr. Noyes, the minister, who lived on Elm Street just below the east corner of the great square. But they could not have been many hours in the town before being shown the field (where Osborn Hall now stands) upon which the trustees were eagerly planning to put up a college house. It was this house for which two years later the name "Yale College" was to be proposed, in honor of a certain wealthy old man in England, who had given something, and vaguely promised more, to the young institution.

An institution it scarcely was as yet, in any modern sense; rather a group of scholars, younger or older, with serious but narrowly academic ambitions. No college house yet existed, no center for the students except the lodgings of Tutor Johnson and the house of Mr. Noyes. The Commencement, that year and for many years after, was held in the meeting-house on the Green.

Such, then, were the conditions that met the Yale Freshman of 1716:—a little town of farmers and mechanics, an absent rector (Mr. Andrew, living at Milford), two tutors to work under, and a few dozen books to work with, chiefly Greek and Latin classics and theology. And his equipment matched these conditions. He had himself grown up to his present fifteen or sixteen years on some Connecticut farm, and his "all-round training" might have challenged comparison with that of the modern Yale boy, but his academic preparation would seem to us narrow. Narrow—and solitary. He had usually received it, if he came of a line of scholars, from his father, or if not, from some nearby clergyman. Besides learning to read and write English—by no means a general achievement then—he had studied Greek and Latin and perhaps Hebrew, had read some Latin theological books and some logic and rhetoric, and a little mathematics. Of natural science, as we understand the term, he had none, for the "physicks" of that day was chiefly a compendium of popular superstitions. Certain of Sir Isaac Newton's books—author's copies!—may indeed have been sleeping on the shelves in Dr.

Buckingham's house at Saybrook. Two of them, the *Principia* and the *Optics,* were in Tutor Johnson's possession, but he did not know enough mathematics to understand them, and was spending such leisure as he had in trying to supplement the defects of his early training.

When one surveys the character and circumstances of this little scholar-group at New Haven, it would seem to have promised little more as the center for a great cultural institution than did the other scholar groups at Wethersfield and at Saybrook. But for those gifted with the "prescience of the eve,"—and there were those so endowed,—the promise was clear. Already the first college building was being eagerly planned, a building large enough to hold sixty-six students, large enough to hold the great Saybrook library, large enough to hold, in its assembly room (31 feet by 22), the Commencement throng of students, tutors, trustees, and invited guests. Two years from this time the structure was completed. It was a very long building, very narrow (165 feet by 22), three stories high, and tradition insists that it was painted blue. But tradition also insists that it was a dignified and impressive building, indeed, one of the most dignified and impressive in New England.

To the trustees, to the tutors and the students, it must have been much more than an impressive and dignified building. It was the great Connecticut College. It was the outward and visible sign of their loyalty, their hopes, and their ideals. To us, looking back, it is Yale University.

THE EXPANSION OF YALE
INTO A UNIVERSITY

By

WILLIAM BEEBE

One of the first acts of President Stiles after his election was to draw up a plan for a university. The manuscript of this plan, which has never been published, is in his own handwriting and begins as follows:

Dec. 1, 1777.

PLAN OF A UNIVERSITY

A Seminary for the Educ^a of Youth in the Latin & Greek Classics only, is but a *Grammar School:* when furnished with academical Instruction or Tuition as in Logic, Geography, Philosophy, Astron^y, Ethics & the rest of the Liberal Arts & Sciences, it becomes a *College:* when in addition to the Languages & Liberal Arts, it exhibits Instruction in higher Learning & espy in the 3 Learned Professions of Div^y Law & Physic, it rises into a University. Yale College would be furnished with Advantages for an Educ^a in universal Literature, if the following Plan should be completed. Officers of Instruction

The President & ⎱ for Languages, Ethics, Lib^l Arts & Sciences.
Three Tutors ⎰
Professor of Divinity—Rev^d Dr. Dagget
Professor of Ecc. History—President
Professor of Law
Professor of Physic
Professor of Math^s & Nat^l Phil. Revd W. Strong
Professor of Hebrew & the Oriental Languages
Professor of Oratory & belles Lettres & civil History

Instruction in all these Branches of Literature has hitherto been given in Yale College, except in *Law & Physic.* It is greatly to be desired that the Utility of these two professorships might appear to the public in so strong a Light as to induce either the *State* or *Individuals* of Opulence & Liberality to make the Endowments necessary for their Support, regulating such additional Institutions to the mutual Satisfaction of the *Corporation* & the *Founders* and consistent with the original Constitution of the College.

Nearly a century passed and four presidents fulfilled their terms of office before the plan of President Stiles received official recognition as an accomplished fact. In March, 1872, five months after the inauguration of President Porter, the following resolution was passed by the Corporation:

Whereas, Yale College has, by the successive establishment of the various departments of instruction, attained to the form of a university:

Resolved, that it be recognized as comprising the four departments of which a university is commonly understood to consist, viz., the Departments of Theology, of Law, of Medicine, and of Philosophy and the Arts.

The University which was thus officially born after a prenatal period of 170 years did not receive baptism until the first year of President Dwight's administration, when in March, 1887, an Act passed the General Assembly of the State authorizing the use of the title "Yale University" instead of that previously used, "The President and Fellows of Yale College," but without invalidating the former title. The one marked step of progress toward the University goal taken during Porter's administration was that of establishing the elective system in the Academic Department, a step whose importance was realized by few of either its supporters or its opponents in the long and ardent discussion that preceded its adoption. The curriculum of the Sheffield Scientific School was from the first well suited to the University idea, but that of the Academic Department was not, and as the elective system developed at Harvard the discrepancy between the two departments became continually more embarrassing. By this change in the Academic Department, inaugurated in 1884, the

A View of the BUILDINGS of YALE COLLEGE, New Haven.

THE EXPANSION OF YALE

road was prepared for President Dwight to proceed comfortably towards a coordinate and harmonious development, and under the stimulus of his sagacity and executive ability the lethargy into which Yale had fallen during the eighties rapidly disappeared.

To appreciate the influence on the development of the University idea of this change in one department, it is necessary to remember how large a part of the University that department then was. In numbers, prestige, endowment and income it surpassed all the other departments taken together. It alone was solvent, and the deficits in income of other departments were commonly made good from its revenues.

The readiest means of reckoning superficially the progress of thirty years is by an examination of the University Catalogue and the Treasurer's Reports. In 1885 the College Catalogue was a thin, yellow-covered pamphlet of about one hundred pages, from which standard it had not varied appreciably for many years. At present the General Catalogue of the University contains one thousand pages, and it is supplemented by about a dozen special reports of the several departments, each of which is usually larger than the sole catalogue of 1885. Any analysis of this mass of literature, representing the development of the twenty-nine years of the legally constituted life of the University, is far beyond the limits of this chapter, but a few significant summaries may be presented.

	1886-7	1899-1900	1915-16
Number of enrolled students	1,134	2,517	3,267
Number of undergraduates ..	849	1,795	2,499
Instructors of all grades	112	242	494
Instructors of first grade	62	80	141
Income-producing endowment	$2,990,000.	6,120,000.	19,200,000.
Income	341,000.	727,000.	1,650,000.
Salaries paid to instructors ..	198,000.	357,000.	740,000.
Per cent used for salaries ...	58	49	45

The increase of endowment is shown not more by a five-fold gain in income than by the enlarged plant of the University. More important than new departments and great groups of buildings, completed and projected, is the spirit that informs them. The vigor of a university's life is most evident in its library, and the growth of the Yale Library and its accessories, the Elizabethan Club, the University Press, and the *Yale Review,* gives satisfactory evidence of the vigor of this life.

Equally important to the life and health of a university is the zeal of its alumni. The zeal of the Yale Alumni, always strong, is changing noticeably from the sentimental to the practical—a change which dates from the Bicentennial Celebration. More than half of all living Alumni came up to that Celebration and found in it a Pentecost whose inspiration extended through them to the absent portion, and it has found its expression in the establishment and rapid growth of the Alumni Fund, in the federation of Yale Clubs, in the Alumni Advisory Board, and in the numbers who come to New Haven yearly on Alumni Day (Feb. 22d) to study at first hand the mechanism of the University in actual operation; and it receives a strong impetus from the Exercises of each successive Commencement—a function whose dignity and power we now reckon as a factor of large import in our University life. In placing a value on the ceremonial side of Yale life we pay a tribute to the character of its originator—the lamented Schwab. It is ennobling because it is the work of a noble nature.

As we look to the future, three features of development show themselves as essential to the realization of the ideal of Yale as a University.

First, the development of the Graduate School of study leading to the degree of Doctor of Philosophy. A hopeful beginning has been made, but the first essential to a larger measure of success is the endowment or support from university funds of professorships with salaries large enough to attract the foremost scholars in special departments. The next essential is concentration on a few departments where we have the opportunity to lead the field. The third essential is the development of a dormitory system for graduate students and of an esprit de corps among them.

Next, a substantial increase in salaries. Thirty years ago the amount paid for salaries of instructors was 58% of the income of the University. Now it is 45%. With the development of the University the cost of maintenance, administration and other overhead charges has greatly increased, but Yale will automatically retire to the second rank if she cannot offer salaries that will attract to her the best teachers and the foremost scholars, not only from other universities but also from business and the professions.

Last. Some means must be found to increase the efficiency of the undergraduate students. Three-fourths of our students are, and are likely to be, undergraduates. Our prestige, our esprit, and our atmosphere of scholarship has always depended and, we may hope, will always depend on them. At present the importance of intellectual development is little appreciated by the average undergraduate. Whether the absorption in extra-curriculum activities of which much, but not too much, is continually said, be the cause or effect of this indifference is a question to be carefully studied; but whatever the diagnosis, the cure of this malady is the most serious problem confronting the Faculties, the Corporation, and the Alumni.

YALE COLLEGE

By

HENRY PARKS WRIGHT

Yale College began as the "Collegiate School" of Connecticut, when Connecticut was a small colony of the English Crown and when the population of New England was considerably less than the present population of the city of New Haven. Until 1716 it was located nominally at Saybrook, where Commencements were held. During this period it had a feeble existence, with never more than thirty students in any one term. It was not called Yale College till two years after its removal to New Haven, when, having received substantial gifts from Governor Elihu Yale, it took his name.

For more than a half century all the instruction was given by the President, with the assistance of tutors who served for short periods. The only teachers added during the first one hundred years were a professor of divinity, and a professor of mathematics and natural philosophy. Under the administration of the first President Dwight, three young graduates of the College were made permanent professors, in mathematics, in ancient languages, and in chemistry. By the gradual addition of new studies, and later by the introduction of the elective system, the original limited curriculum has been expanded into the present plan of study, with about two hundred and fifty College and University professors and instructors.

From very early times, graduates of the College sometimes remained to pursue advanced studies especially in divinity. To provide opportunity for the study of the professions and of subjects not included in the college curriculum, other schools have grown up around the original academical institution which, still retaining the name Yale College, given to it in 1718, now forms one of the nine schools that make up Yale University.

The removal of Yale to New Haven has proved fortunate. The collegiate school which was brought here has become a great university; New Haven has grown to be a city large enough to afford the advantages and the protection which a university should have; and with the facilities of modern travel, it is situated at a convenient distance from the city, which, though small two hundred years ago, has become the metropolis of the nation.

Though the chief aim of the College has been mental and moral training and sound learning, largely through the influence of other departments of the University and by their coöperation, it has added to its courses of instruction subjects of a practical and of a vocational nature, with special reference to future professions or pursuits. Founded and for nearly a century governed solely by clergymen of one denomination, it has grown more and more liberal and has become non-sectarian. Narrow at one time in the theological tests required of its teachers, it stands to-day for entire freedom of thought and of speech.

The Yale undergraduate life of the first century was quite unlike that of to-day. For nearly seventy years the names of students were arranged in the catalogue, not alphabetically but according to the social rank of the families to which they belonged; and one penalty for certain misdemeanors was "Degrading," that is, placing a student's name lower on this list. By the early college laws, undergraduates were required to uncover their heads in the college yard when the President or a tutor was there, and also when either was in sight in any other place; students were directed not to use the English tongue in conversation with one another, but to talk in Latin; any Freshman was obliged to go on any reasonable errand for any student in an upper class, and was liable to punishment if he refused so to do. One penalty for obstinate behavior toward the President or a tutor was: "Being deprived of the liberty of sending freshmen." Until the close of the first century a fine was the common penalty for irregularity of attendance or for misdemeanors. Absence from prayers at one time was punished by a fine of twopence. If a student went more than two miles from college without leave, he was liable to a fine of two shillings. Professor Benjamin Silliman, when a Freshman, was fined sixpence by President Stiles for kicking a football in the college yard. Up to the middle of the last century, morning and evening prayers were held each day, the time of morning prayers being generally five in the summer and at sunrise in the winter. A burlesque of the old yellow-covered Yale catalogue expressed the students' view: "Prayers are held sometime during the night, generally toward morning."

The attitude of the students toward the Faculty has not always been as cordial and friendly as it is now. In very early times there were special laws against raising scandalous reports about the President and tutors and calling them hypocrites or unconverted, or making an assault on their persons. The Faculty were strict and unyielding, and the students sometimes obstinate. The feeling of opposition on the part of the students culminated in 1828 and in 1830 in two serious rebellions known as the "Bread and Butter Rebellion" and the "Conic Sections Rebellion." In the latter, forty-four members of one class, refusing to submit to new requirements of the Faculty regarding recitations in Conic Sections, were permanently separated from college, and appeals for their restoration were unavailing. That event settled the question of Faculty authority at Yale for all time. Since then there has been no combination of students to resist it, and the spirit of rebellion would now be wholly foreign to the place. President Day said to a delegation of students who came to him to object to the demands of the Faculty: "Yale College is an absolute monarchy." To-day Faculty and students work together harmoniously. The student body to a great degree governs itself, under the direction of the Faculty. The characteristic spirit of the College is one of respect for authority and of willing obedience. Outside activities, as long as they do not interfere with study or with college order, are left, with some

AN EARLY NINETEENTH CENTURY VIEW OF YALE COLLEGE AND THE GREEN

Faculty oversight, to the students themselves. With the privilege of greater freedom and responsibility, the general tone of college life has steadily improved.

The value of the Yale training is shown by what its graduates have been and by what they have done. The purpose of the founders of Yale College was to fit men for public service in church and state. The College has abundantly fulfilled this purpose. Among its nearly eighteen thousand graduates have been eminent theologians and preachers, who have greatly influenced the religious thought of the country; educational leaders, who have helped to lay the foundations of many of the best American colleges and universities; great lawyers, and jurists, and statesmen. Yale men have been especially prominent in public life and have filled with honor positions of the highest responsibility. They appeared conspicuous among the members of the Continental Congress, among the signers of the Declaration of Independence, and among the members of the Convention that framed the national Constitution. Their names are found on the lists of Presidents and Vice-Presidents of the United States, of Cabinet officers, of Justices and Chief Justices of the Supreme Court, of Foreign Ambassadors, of United States Senators and Congressmen, of Governors of states and of foreign possessions, and of the holders of every office of distinction known to the American people.

The graduates of Yale have been characterized by a spirit of loyalty, of self-sacrifice, and of service. They have carried the influence of Yale to every part of the nation and to lands beyond the seas. Wherever there has been a great work to do for civic or social reform, for public and private morals or health, for religion, or for humanity, Yale men have been found among the leaders. The Yale spirit is the spirit of Nathan Hale, who, with so much to live for, gave up all and met death manfully and fearlessly in the service of his country.

THE SHEFFIELD SCIENTIFIC SCHOOL

By

RUSSELL H. CHITTENDEN

What is now the Sheffield Scientific School had its beginning seventy years ago, at a time when general interest in the natural and physical sciences was being aroused through the successful efforts of European students, especially many eminent men in Germany, in applying the facts of science to the arts, agriculture, and the industries of the world. It was evident that a new era in education was at hand, in which the experimental sciences were destined to play an important part, and in 1846 there was established at Yale—as a part of the new "Department of Philosophy and the Arts"—a "School of Applied Chemistry," for the purpose of practical instruction in the application of science to the arts and agriculture.

This was followed in 1852 by a "School of Engineering," with Professor William A. Norton as Professor of Civil Engineering. At this time there were enrolled in the Department of Philosophy and the Arts forty-six students, quite a number of whom held a bachelor's degree. Of these, twenty-six were enrolled as students in Engineering, while sixteen were designated as students in Applied Chemistry, thus indicating that in these early years the two Schools of Chemistry and Engineering furnished practically all the life of the Department of Philosophy and the Arts. Further, each year brought out more clearly that many men who had not had a college training desired the opportunity to pursue scientific studies, and it is to be noted that in 1854, formal announcement was made that the degree of Bachelor of Philosophy would be conferred by the President and

Fellows upon students in the Department of Philosophy and the Arts after being connected with the Department two years and passing a satisfactory examination in three branches of study. This marked the formal movement for distinctly undergraduate courses, which in 1858 culminated in a definite organization, the "Yale Scientific School," under the Department of Philosophy and the Arts, commissioned to give systematic instruction in Natural Science, Chemistry, Agriculture and Engineering. For graduate students pursuing higher courses in Science followed by original investigation in some chosen field of work, the degree of Doctor of Philosophy was provided, and it is worthy of note that the award of this higher degree in America was first made here.

During these years a citizen of New Haven, Mr. Joseph E. Sheffield, had become interested in the growing Scientific School and had manifested his interest by successive gifts of money, which were greatly needed. In 1860, he purchased and presented to the School the building now known as Sheffield Hall, which for twelve years or more served as its only home, though at that time it seemed a commodious palace compared with the old president's house in which the analytical laboratory was first established. Mr. Sheffield likewise at this time gave the sum of fifty thousand dollars to the President and Fellows of the College for the endowment of the School, and in recognition of his generous gifts the Corporation changed its name to the Sheffield Scientific School.

During these years of growth and development the value of scientific education was gradually gaining ground, in spite of "conflicts between Science and Religion" and in spite of the dominating influence of classical learning. The claims of modern language, of classical English, of Economics, of Commercial Geography, of the Social Sciences, were likewise presenting themselves as worthy of consideration in a scheme which was confessedly concerned with the present rather than with the remote past. Consequently, we find the School gradually enlarging its scope, and in the year 1869-70 there were six distinct courses

of study scheduled leading to the bachelor's degree, in which
the Freshman year was common to all.   1. Chemistry and
Metallurgy, 2. Civil Engineering and Mechanics, 3. Mining and
Metallurgy, 4. Agriculture, 5. Natural History and Geology,
6. Select Course in scientific and literary studies.   In the year
1869-70, the total registration of students in the School was one
hundred and thirty-nine; twenty-six graduate students, twenty-
five Seniors, thirty-eight Juniors, thirty-eight Freshmen, and
twelve special students.

In 1871, at the request of Mr. Sheffield, certain professors of
the School, with other friends of the institution, organized themselves into a body corporate under the laws of the state of Connecticut, and this incorporation of the Board of Trustees of
the Sheffield Scientific School was confirmed by Act of the
General Assembly in 1882.   The original incorporators were
George J. Brush, Daniel C. Gilman, William P. Trowbridge, John
S. Beach, William Walter Phelps, and Charles J. Sheffield.   At
once, Mr. Sheffield deeded to this Board of Trustees a piece of
land on Prospect Street and erected thereon North Sheffield Hall,
the second building for the work of the School.   In 1889, after
the death of Mrs. Sheffield, all the land on Sheffield Square, with
the mansion house thereon, came into the hands of the Trustees,
and this, with the other bequests and gifts of Mr. Sheffield,
represented more than a million dollars given to the School.
Small wonder that the men of his generation, like the men of the
present day, looked upon him as a man whom it was a delight
to acknowledge and honor.

To-day, the Sheffield Scientific School is quite a different thing
from the child of seventy or even forty years ago.   It now stands
as one of the conspicuous schools of the University, with a teaching staff of one hundred and sixty-three.   The alumni of the
School number six thousand, five thousand three hundred and
ninety of whom are living.   Each year shows a body of undergraduate students numbering one thousand, more or less.   Of
graduate students, candidates for higher engineering degrees,
there are each year sixty-five to seventy, while from the Grad-

uate School of the University one hundred and twenty-five take one or more courses of advanced study in the School. In addition, one hundred and twenty or more students from other schools of the University come to the Scientific School for instruction, thus making a grand total of nearly thirteen hundred under instruction each year. There are thirteen distinct buildings— donated mainly by graduates and other friends of the institution—in which the work of the School is carried on, including well-equipped laboratories of Mining and Metallurgy (The Hammond Laboratory), Mechanical Engineering (Mason Laboratory), and Electrical Engineering, in addition to the University laboratories of Botany, Zoology and Physics, in which it shares with the College and Graduate School. There is a dormitory square—Vanderbilt Square—on which several beautiful dormitory buildings have been erected through the generosity of Mr. Frederick W. Vanderbilt, of the Class of 1876 S.; also a social hall for the social and religious life of the students, known as Byers Memorial Hall.

The Board of Trustees of the Sheffield Scientific School holds property valued at over three million dollars, while the Treasurer of the University holds for the benefit of the School more than three-quarters of a million dollars. Riches, truly, but by no means adequate to meet the present-day needs of the Sheffield Scientific School if she is to keep pace with the ever-increasing demands for specialized instruction in all the sciences that have application to the arts and industries of this generation.

At present there are twelve distinct undergraduate courses leading to the bachelor's degree, viz.: Chemistry; Mathematics and Physics; Civil Engineering; Mechanical Engineering; Electrical Engineering; Mining Engineering; Metallurgical Engineering; three Biological Courses including Physiological Chemistry, Bacteriology and Hygiene; Selected Studies in Language, Literature, History and the Natural and Social Sciences; Studies preparatory to Forestry. In addition to these, there are two-year graduate courses in the various branches of Engineering leading to the higher engineering degrees; two-year graduate courses in Economic Geology; Applied Chemistry; Metallography; Applied Biology; Bacteriology and Hygiene; and Applied Biochemistry—all leading to the degree of Master of Science; and a graduate course in Business Administration. Lastly, in nearly every field of science there are advanced courses of instruction leading to the degree of Doctor of Philosophy.

THE GRADUATE SCHOOL

By

HENRY W. FARNAM

The present Graduate School has grown out of the courses for graduate students first offered at Yale in 1846. This was a small beginning, but it was a significant step, both in the history of Yale and in the history of higher education in the United States. For Yale was the pioneer in this expansion of the work of the college into the work of a real university. This was recognized by the Carnegie Foundation for the Advancement of Teaching, which says in a report on the evolution of the American type of university: "The honor of having established the first creditable course of study for the degree of Doctor of Philosophy is due to Yale."

In the early days the courses were few and informal, and it was not until 1861 that those who pursued them might look forward to getting as their reward the degree of Doctor of Philosophy. The college had, it is true, for many years conferred the degree of Master of Arts, but not for scholarship, and the only requisites for this honor were that a student must have lived for three years after graduation and have been able during that time both to maintain a good moral character and to accumulate a sum of $5, with which to pay for his sheepskin. In 1874 this method of award was abandoned, and the degree was henceforth given only for scholarly attainments.

After the close of the Civil War there was a marked growth in the cultivation of scientific studies, and both the courses and the number of students in the graduate department increased rapidly. In 1871 the circular which was issued upon the accession of President Porter contained a list of but 23 courses. In

1886, upon the accession of President Dwight, this number had increased to 61, and in 1892, to a total of 207, of which 94 were undergraduate courses open to graduates, and 113 were graduate courses. In this year a more formal organization was given to the department by the creation of the office of dean and by the appointment of Professor Arthur T. Hadley to this position. Upon the accession of Professor Andrew W. Phillips to the deanship in 1895, the department was installed in an office, modest to be sure, and plain, but still an office of its own at 90 High Street. Since that time the number of courses and of students has increased substantially. The total number of courses, graduate and undergraduate, scheduled in the catalogue for 1915-16 was nearly 450, and the total number of students, 409, of whom 63 were graduate students in the Sheffield Scientific School.

The Graduate School has been a progressive department of the university from the very beginning. Its early history was closely connected with the history of the Scientific School, which indeed was almost identical with it in the beginning, and as recently as 1870 the courses of graduate instruction were grouped with the Sheffield Scientific School in what was sonorously called the Department of Philosophy and the Arts. The Graduate School was also the first department of the university to admit women as candidates for a degree, and since 1892 they have been freely enrolled in graduate courses leading to the degree of Ph.D. In recent years the Graduate School has opened its doors to teachers not candidates for a degree, who are thus able to broaden their culture without giving up their regular occupation, and there were 118 of them enrolled during the year 1915-16. The number of women in the same year was 108, of whom 81 were entered as teachers and 27 as candidates for the Doctor's degree.

The degrees of Doctor of Philosophy and Master of Arts have long been the two principal degrees conferred for graduate studies, but the requirements for them have been so raised, that they now stand for something very different from that for which they stood forty years ago. In the case of the doctor's degree the principle has always been to look for quality rather than for any specific period of study, but it is significant that, whereas formerly a student was expected, according to the statement in the catalogue, to spend two or more years in preparation for this degree, since 1910 three years have been required, and that now the thesis must be printed, either in whole or in part. The requirements for the degree of Master of Arts have likewise been raised. Until 1912 only one year of study in residence was required. Since that time a student must have spent two years in graduate study, either at Yale or elsewhere, and must also prepare an essay. In the same year the administration of the degree, which had formerly been in charge of the College faculty, was entrusted more consistently to the faculty of the Graduate School. The degrees given for graduate study in natural science and engineering are, however, still conferred upon the recommendation of the Governing Board of the Sheffield Scientific School, and these degrees have increased materially in number and in scope of late years. In addition to the degree of Civil Engineer, first conferred in 1860, and of Mechanical Engineer, first conferred in 1873, we now have degrees in electrical engineering, mining engineering, and metallurgical engineering, as well as the more general degree of Master of Science, while in 1915 the Scientific School established graduate courses in business administration to which only graduates are admitted, but for which at present no degree is conferred. A volume issued in 1916 by the Graduate School gives the following summaries:

TABLE OF DOCTORATES BY PERIODS

	Men	Women	Total
1861 to 1869	16	0	16
Decade 1870 to 1879	47	0	47
Decade 1880 to 1889	40	0	40
Decade 1890 to 1899	186	31	217
Decade 1900 to 1909	290	42	332
1910 to 1915	175	21	196
	754	94	848

TABLE OF DOCTORATES BY DEPARTMENTS

	Chronological rank in respect to first degrees conferred	Year in which the degree was first conferred	Number of Men who received the degree	Number of Women who received the degree	Total number who received the degree	Number deceased	Dissertations published
Classical Philology, etc.	1	1861	90	11	101	13	35
Physics	1	1861	43	0	43	2	29
Mathematics	2	1862	52	10	62	5	35
Chemistry	3	1866	99	3	102	8	93
Geological Sciences	4	1867	49	2	51	1	43
Zoology and Comparative Anatomy	4	1867	14	1	15	0	14
Philosophy and Education	5	1874	83	7	90	4	34
English	6	1875	72	34	106	5	69
Economics, Anthropology, etc.	7	1877	50	3	53	2	24
Physiological Chemistry, etc.	8	1880	48	6	54	1	49
History	9	1882	48	12	60	3	29
Semitic Languages	10	1888	48	1	49	7	18
Romance Languages	11	1894	14	3	17	1	7
Germanic Languages	12	1896	20	4	24	1	8
Botany	13	1899	8	2	10	0	10
Department undetermined		1861	11	0	11	6	
			749	99	848	59	497

In connection with the Graduate School and as an important part of its work a large number of scientific clubs have been formed in the various departments. These furnish an opportunity for the reading of papers and for discussions in which both students and teachers take part. The meetings are often held in a special seminar room in which the departmental library is shelved, and in some cases merge into seminar work. These clubs are stimulating alike to students and faculty, and are of great assistance, especially in the preliminary stages of the preparation of a thesis. Their work is in a sense supplemented by the various periodicals such as the *Yale Review,* the *American Journal of Science,* and other more highly specialized publications, edited by members of the faculty, while the Connecticut Academy of Arts and Sciences and the Yale University Press often furnish a convenient medium of publication.

Of the various departments of the university the Graduate School is perhaps the one which is least known to the great body of the students. It has no sports or social functions, it has not even buildings devoted specifically to its use, and the dean's office is so inconspicuous as to invite an underestimate of the importance of the department. This is natural in a school which emphasizes quality more than numbers. A word should, therefore, be said regarding the purposes of a graduate department. Its specific functions are to promote research, to train future members of the faculty, and to enable the university to play its part in filling other public or semi-public positions requiring specialized training.

In developing her graduate courses to meet these new demands, Yale is but carrying out the function so well expressed in the charter of 1701, when the college was expressly founded as a place "wherein Youth may be instructed in the Arts & Sciences who thorough the blessing of Almighty God may be fitted for Publick employment both in Church & Civil State."

YALE IN MEDICINE

By

HARVEY CUSHING

The eccentric Charles C. Colton, sometime canon of Salisbury, once pointed out the difficulties of authorship in a discourse entitled *Lacon, or Many Things in a Few Words.* As the Pageant itself tells its story by selected scenes, so must these essays on Yale relate their chief incidents with laconic brevity.

After the removal of the school from Saybrook two hundred years ago, Yale remained but a college for a full century more. The original charter promised such instruction as would fit Youth for "Publick Employment both in Church and Civil State," but the Connecticut pastors who drafted this early document could little have suspected that a department of Medicine was to be the entering wedge to split the "Academic Institution" into what would become a university. At this point, early in the Presidency of the elder Timothy Dwight, the story of *Medicine in Yale* begins. The story of *Yale in Medicine,* however, is twice as long.

During the colonial days in Connecticut, the practice of Medicine was largely a priestly profession, the torch, as Thacher suggests, possibly having been handed on to the ministers of the colony by its first governor, the younger Winthrop, who had made of Medicine an avocation. Be this as it may, many a reverend minister of Yale after some sort of medical tutelage came to care alike for the ills both of body and soul, and not a few became more renowned as doctors than as presbyters. Famous among these clerical physicians of the early days were Phineas Fiske of 1704 and Jonathan Dickinson of 1706, who later became Princeton's first president and was author of the first medical publication by a graduate of Yale. But the outstanding name remains that of Dickinson's classmate, the Reverend Jared Eliot, "the first physician of his day," Fellow of the Royal Society, and as many-sided as was his friend Benjamin Franklin.

Eliot's influence can be traced by his pupils and their pupils through the century. One, his son-in-law Benjamin Gale (1733), made a noteworthy contribution to the medicine of the time. Another was the industrious Jared Potter (1760) of Wallingford. He in turn had medical apprentices, one of the first being the celebrated Lemuel Hopkins (1784, Hon.),—poet, physician, patriot, one of the "Hartford wits." The lexicographer, Noah Webster (1778), another of the famous Hartford group when Hartford was "denominated the Athens of America," may be claimed by Medicine for his great treatise on epidemic and pestilential diseases. Still another was Mason F. Cogswell (1780), leading surgeon of the state, who established the first asylum for the deaf and dumb and whose relation to the founding of the medical school properly brings us to the story of Medicine in Yale.

In 1802 the elder Dwight, sagacious in his choice of young faculty members, filled the chair of Natural Science by a recent graduate who was to become the leading American scientist of his day. It was largely at Benjamin Silliman's instigation that the momentous step of establishing a separate medical department was taken. Though six other schools were in operation, it was apparent that, if the practice of medicine in Connecticut was to be improved, such a school was needed there also. A well-organized state medical society, largely influenced by Yale graduates, was already in existence and had received the statutory privilege of conferring degrees. Under the joint auspices of this society and the College, the Medical Institution in 1810 was finally incorporated. Such a foundation is unique in the history of American medical schools, most of which have been organized at the outset as private ventures by a group of interested persons. At Yale the department was born within the college and inherited its blue laws. Students were not permitted to assault, wound, or strike the President, or maliciously break his windows or doors without fear of expulsion, and they perforce abstained from hallooing in studying time, nor were they permitted to wear women's apparel, or pick locks, or commit like crimes. Then too, there was compulsory attendance at prayers, and dormitories and a commons—features which we might well imitate to-day,— were provided.

The original faculty, comprising the aged Eneas Munson (1753) and his understudy, Eli Ives (1799), Jonathan Knight (1808), Nathan Smith, and Benjamin Silliman (1796), was of such distinction as to bring to the school during its first two decades a celebrity second to none. Though Silliman, whose *Journal* long made Yale the center of scientific activity in the country, and Knight, twice chosen president of the American Medical Association, each served for the unusual period of fifty-one years, the fame of the school unquestionably radiated from the person of Nathan Smith who for sixteen years was at once Professor of the Theory and Practice of Physic, Surgery, and Obstetrics. No less through his many successful pupils of the period at Yale than through his direct descendants can the medical influence of this one man be traced throughout the land to the present day.

After its brilliant start the prosperity of the school declined, for competitive institutions rapidly came into being under more metropolitan auspices. Then too there was sore need of a general hospital as an auxiliary to the school, and the promise of this has come only with the present century, in which the time-honored institution, which has ever maintained a high standard despite its small enrollment, bids fair to show a revival of the prestige it enjoyed a hundred years ago. Meanwhile, with Yale's rapid growth in science during the latter half of the century, Medicine was far from neglected and, with the founding of the Scientific School, pre-medical courses were outlined with the express object of securing a thorough undergraduate preparation for its pursuit. Through these courses during the last forty years, and particularly through that in physiological chemistry under Russell H. Chittenden (1875), there has gone a succession of men who have carried Yale's name into Medicine.

Indeed Yale's chief medical influence during her past century has been exerted by her graduates in the Arts or Sciences. Of many examples, two may perhaps be singled out. One concerns the spread of Medicine in the far East, the other the more recent development in medical education at home.

A link between the clerical physicians of the eighteenth century and her many foreign missionaries of to-day was Peter Parker, he who "opened the gates of China at the point of his lancet." After graduating in 1831 he took a medical degree and studied theology preparatory for his object in life—to use medicine as a means of introducing Christianity in the Orient. Though not actually the first physician in China, he was the first to prepare himself as a medical missionary. He founded the famous Canton Hospital in 1835, gained the confidence of the leading Chinese, had many promising native pupils, and ultimately became United States Commissioner. Chinese students began to come to Yale, the celebrated Yung Wing (1854) being the first to graduate. So Parker's career in the East has doubtless had much to do with the present successful graft of Yale on that ancient center of Chinese culture, Changsha. Here at Ya-li a young graduate of 1897 and a Chinese medical graduate of 1909 have together organized a most promising school of medicine, the forerunner of other institutions which will profoundly influence the development of this far country.

Another movement which has revolutionized medical education and in which Yale graduates have played a leading rôle began with the founding of the Johns Hopkins University and is due in large part to its first president, Daniel C. Gilman (1852), who for a time was the actual superintendent and director of the most vigorous branch of that notable institution, its hospital and medical school. Wise in his choice of men, Gilman set the school revolving around a Yale graduate of 1870, and it has continued so to revolve for the past thirty years, with an ever widening influence which has deeply affected medical science and medical teaching over the entire country. Several of the men who have received their training or doctorate there have brought back to the school in New Haven much of the stimulating spirit of that place.   At the present time the four university Professorships of the Johns Hopkins School under the William H. Welch Endowment of the General Education Board are held by Yale graduates of the classes of 1870, 1874, 1892, and 1894, and through Gilman to them Yale may take unto herself the satisfaction of an academic parentage.

A favorite quotation with President Gilman was Richard Horne's line:

'Tis always morning somewhere in the world—

and after its period of repose we may expect the Yale Medical School in her turn to arise strengthened for a new day in which Medicine in Yale may come again to outrival what Yale has been in Medicine.

YALE IN DIVINITY

By

BENJAMIN W. BACON

The services of Yale to theology have been preëminent, as was to be anticipated from the design of her founders. These services may be grouped according to the two centuries of her existence. Throughout the eighteenth century and the first two decades of the nineteenth no separate School of Religion existed. In the opening years of the nineteenth, plans had already been formed for a separate Department of Theology by President Timothy Dwight, himself the leading theologian of his time; but two further decades were required to bring these plans to their fruition. Until the founding in 1822 of the present School of Religion the college itself had been from its foundation in 1701 a School of Religion, making the study of theology the culminating point of its curriculum. In this period inevitably its services to theology were predominantly the contributions of individual men, Jonathan Edwards, one of the earliest and still the most illustrious of its graduates, leading the van.

The second century of service, which to-day in its turn is rounding to completion, is one of research and training under the university system of separate departments for the chief lines of cultural development. Names of great individual leaders of thought and activity naturally do not cease to appear. They are even increased in number. But over and above the individual services of graduates of the college and School of Theology such as Horace Bushnell, Peter Parker, and Theodore Thornton Munger, there must be reckoned the contribution of the School itself. In the eighteenth century the theology distinctive of Yale, indeed distinctive of America, was the reconstructed Calvinism of Jonathan Edwards. This was called "the New England Theology." It was in substance an adjustment of the too *a priori* system of Calvin to the rigorous realism of John Locke by whom Edwards was profoundly influenced. The modifications introduced by Hopkins, Bellamy, West, Smalley, Emmons, Dwight, and the younger Edwards, were intended as "improvements," not as refutations, and belonged like the system of Edwards in the field of the psychology of religion. Though designated "the New England Theology" it was really a product of Yale; for, as Secretary Stokes remarks, in his *Memorials of Eminent Yale Men,* "Of the eight leaders who created this 'system' and handed it down with their own modifications from generation to generation, all but one were graduates, . . and the other, the younger Edwards, was a 'grandson' of Yale and a New Haven pastor."

A different line of theological development, but one in which the fame of Yale was destined later to stand no less high, is marked even in these early days by the name of Moses Stuart of the Class of 1799, "the founder of modern biblical scholarship in America." What Ezra Stiles had done for an earlier generation, what William R. Harper did for our own, Moses Stuart did for his, and perpetuated the work by his writings and the work of those whom he taught at Andover.

But the attention of the world was still concentrated upon theology proper, rather than the problems of biblical and historical criticism for which the linguistic studies of "Moses Stuart—the man who unfettered religious thought in America" were to prepare the way. The new adaptation of Calvinism which was to meet more effectively than any other this side the Atlantic the sweeping revelations of physical science and the doctrine of evolution was known as "the New Haven theology." This designation was undoubtedly framed to distinguish the more progressive branch of New England Theology represented by Nathaniel W. Taylor and his associates in the newly formed Theological Department of the University from the conservative, represented by Dr. Bennet Tyler (B.A. Yale 1804) and his associates in the Seminary

I. EDWARDS, PRES.

Trotter sculp.

Publish'd as the Act directs March 7th 1783

From an original Picture in the possession of the Revd Dr Erskine Edinburgh.

JONATHAN EDWARDS

Class of 1720

formed at East Windsor and later removed to Hartford.   Both
the progressive and the reactionary types of New England theology were therefore, in a sense, products of Yale.   It was the
progressive, however, which continued to be representative of the
University and remained in vital relation to it.

From the founding of the Department until his death in 1858
Nathaniel W. Taylor was so much the central figure of the Yale
School of Divinity that its type of thought, characterized by the
doctrines of the moral government of God, and of the reality of
evil (both physical and moral) as incidental to the best possible
universe, might well have borne his name, as its predecessor had
borne the name of Edwards.   But the theology of Dr. Taylor
was justly called "New Haven" theology; for it had a continuity
in two directions not practicable to the earlier time.   The New
Haven theology was the joint work of a group of men including
Fitch and Goodrich within the school itself.   Moreover it
was defended, improved, and supplemented by a group of
theologians both within and without the school whose contributions to the theological thinking of America stand preëminent.
As Edwards marks an epoch for the eighteenth century by his
adjustment of Calvinistic anthropology to the new science of
Locke, so Horace Bushnell, reinterpreting the natural world in
terms of spirit, paved the way for modern theology, and marks the
beginning of a school destined to bring the New England theology
into line with modern science and criticism and the doctrine of
evolution.   Among the graduates who continued Bushnell's work
must be named Theodore T. Munger, author of *The Freedom of
Faith,* and as a graduate of Yale but not of its Divinity School,
Elisha Mulford, author of *The Republic of God.*

The second half of the nineteenth century witnessed a new birth
of the New Haven theology.   With the death of Taylor in 1858,
and the death or retirement of his associates of "the old faculty,"
the Divinity School had experienced a severe decline.   The period
of the Civil War was a period of its reorganization.   To its
faculty were added successively in 1858 Timothy Dwight the
younger as Professor of Sacred Literature, in 1861 George P.

Fisher as Professor of Ecclesiastical History, in 1866 George E. Day as Professor of Hebrew Language and Literature, and in the same year Leonard Bacon, provisionally in the chair of Systematic Theology, subsequently in that of Ecclesiastical Polity. Most important of all the accessions of the period for the development of the New Haven theology was that of Samuel Harris to the chair of Systematic Theology.

It is this later group which gave to the New Haven school of thought its distinctive standing in the latter part of the nineteenth century. Its motto printed on the title-page of its organ, the *New Englander and Yale Review,* was: "Nullius addictus jurare in verba magistri." But this bold rejection of all trammels of tradition did not swerve it from loyal devotion to the vital principles for which the great succession of New England theologians had stood. By their teachings and their writings, as well as by spirit and example, Dwight and Fisher and Harris became the names of light and leading to a great number of representative men of the American pulpit at the close of the nineteenth century. Of the achievements of men now in active service it is impossible to speak. The School still mourns the recent death of George B. Stevens, successor first to Dwight in the chair of New Testament Criticism and Exegesis, later to Samuel Harris in that of Systematic Theology, and that of Edward L. Curtis, successor to George E. Day as Professor of Old Testament Language and Literature and acting Dean.

The opening decades of the twentieth century find the Yale School of Religion in a state of transition similar to that of a century ago. Its scope has been broadened. Its subject is not merely Theology but Religion. Its research is in this whole vast field of human thought and activity. Its training is for no less than five different phases of service in the field, pastoral, missionary, social and philanthropic, educational, and historical or scholastic. The new development has brought new resources to the School and great enlargement of its faculty. The names to be read on the opening pages of its Bulletin are names which to the theological world of to-day speak for themselves.

YALE IN LAW

By

THOMAS THACHER

In 1777, Ezra Stiles (Y. 1746), upon his election to the Presidency of Yale College, urged the importance of including the teaching of law in the scheme of instruction intended to fit "for Publick employment both in Church & Civil State," not, as he said in his "plan of an University," for making lawyers, "but for forming Civilians." Efforts to secure from the Connecticut Assembly an endowment for this purpose failed because the Corporation would not assent to the condition that the Assembly take part in the management of the College. Nothing was accomplished in pursuance of the thought of President Stiles, beyond occasional lectures by him and some recitations before him, until, in 1801, the first professorship of law was created by the appointment of Elizur Goodrich (Y. 1779).

This professorship, filled by Professor Goodrich until 1810, and later by such men as Judge David Daggett (Y. 1783), Governor Clark Bissell (Y. 1806), Governor Henry Dutton (Y. 1818), Hon. Edward J. Phelps (Law School, 1842-3), and now by Ex-President William H. Taft (Y. 1878), has always been devoted to its original purpose, not especially to fit for the practice of the law, but to fit for public service and for citizenship. In 1833 this professorship was named the "Kent Professorship of Law" because of a fund for its support given by friends and admirers of Chancellor Kent, but it still continues a professorship in the Academic Department for undergraduate teaching.

Yale College first became connected with the school out of which grew the present Yale Law School in 1824. The occasion of the starting of this school was the importation, in 1800, of an excellent law library by Seth P. Staples (Y. 1797), a New Haven lawyer. This library drew students to his office, and Mr. Staples "soon found himself the head of a flourishing law school." For twenty years he carried it on alone. In 1820 he called Samuel J. Hitchcock (Y. 1809) to his aid, and in 1824, he turned the school over to Judge David Daggett and Mr. Hitchcock.

At this point Yale College permitted the school to become "affiliated" with it. The only evidence of affiliation in the catalogues of 1824 and 1825 consists of lists of law students, but that of 1826 names Hon. David Daggett as Professor of Law, and describes a law course under him and Samuel J. Hitchcock, Esq. In the same year the Corporation gave Judge Daggett a degree of LL.D. So the affiliation became complete, although the adopted school had to make its own way for many years thereafter without much aid from the general purse; and was not permitted to present candidates for degrees until 1843. When the Staples school was turned over to Judge Daggett and Mr. Hitchcock, the famous Litchfield school was still in its vigor under the charge of James Gould (Y. 1791); but it was, perhaps, already waning, and it came to an end in 1833. The Harvard Law School, started in 1817, did not begin to gather its remarkable strength until after the endowment of the Dane Professorship, accepted by Judge Story in 1829.

The strength of the Law School under Judge Daggett and Mr. Hitchcock (1824-1847) is evidenced by the careers of some of its students, such as Theodore W. Dwight, the eminent law teacher, William Strong and David Davis, Justices of the U. S. Supreme Court, Alphonso Taft and Edwards Pierrepont, Attorneys General of the U. S. (also ministers to Russia and England respectively), Edward J. Phelps, who, during the period of his Kent professorship, represented the United States at the Court of St. James, and also, Governor W. W. Hoppin of Rhode Island, Benjamin D. Silliman of New York, Abraham Browning of New Jersey, Richard D. Hubbard and Charles R. Ingersoll, Governors of Connecticut, and Alexander S. Johnson, Judge of the New York Court of Appeals and later of the U. S. Circuit Court.

From 1847 to 1868 the school was under the care of Governor
Clark Bissell (until 1855) and Governor Henry Dutton, aided
by William L. Storrs (Y. 1814) and Isaac H. Townsend (Y.
1822) in the years 1845 and 1846 and by Thomas B. Osborne
(Y. 1817) from 1855 to 1865. In 1869 the management was
taken up by Simeon E. Baldwin, Johnson T. Platt, and William C.
Robinson, and as a result of their services (those of Governor
Baldwin still continuing) and of the work of Dean Wayland and
Dean Rogers, and of Professor E. J. Phelps, and of William K.
Townsend (Y. 1871, late U. S. Circuit Judge), and of others,
including the members of the present faculty, the school has been
brought into the front rank of the law schools of the country.

Yale's share in the teaching of law through its alumni has
been large. With reference to teaching in the schools, it is only
necessary to recall, in addition to those who have taught in the
Yale Law School, Chancellor Kent (Y. 1781) as a teacher at
Columbia, Judge Gould (Y. 1791) at Litchfield, the first in point
of time, according to Governor Baldwin, "of American Lawyers
who have made the teaching of law the main work of their lives,"
and Theodore W. Dwight (Law School 1841-2), who made the
Columbia Law School famous; but there are others.

With reference to teaching done by books, Yale has a proud
position because of Kent's *Commentaries,* called by Judge Story
"the first judicial classic"; and, also, because of the works of
Zephaniah Swift (Y. 1778), *System of the Laws of Connecticut*
and *Digest of the Laws of Connecticut,* "works of far more than
local interest and frequently termed by writers an American
Blackstone"; and because of such writings as those of President
Theodore Dwight Woolsey (Y. 1820) and Francis Wharton (Y.
1839) on International Law, of Professor James Hadley (Y.
1842) on Roman Law, and of Governor Baldwin on various topics
of law and legal history. Benjamin on *Sales* should, perhaps,
be included, for Judah P. Benjamin studied at Yale for a time.

To the development of the law in the courts by the work of
judges and advocates, Yale has contributed its full share.
Among judges the name of Kent calls for first mention. As

Judge of the Supreme Court of New York for sixteen years and Chancellor for seven years, it is safe to say that he did more than anyone else in this country to develop the law and to make it known to all who would read—called by Judge Dillon "the creator of the equity system of this country."   In the United States Supreme Court have been Henry Baldwin (Y. 1797), William Strong (Y. 1828), David Davis (Law School 1834), Morrison R. Waite (Y. 1837), for fourteen years Chief Justice, William B. Woods (Y. 1845), George Shiras (Y. 1853), Henry B. Brown (Y. 1856), and David J. Brewer (Y. 1856); not to mention Oliver Ellsworth, the second chief-justice, who spent three years at Yale.   The Yale men who have been judges in the lower Federal and in State Courts are too numerous to mention here.

The contribution of the advocates to the development of the law is as great as that of the judges, but one can only suggest a few scenes in which Yale advocates appear, working for the grand purpose of the law, to establish and secure peace, order, liberty, and justice.   In Zenger's trial in 1735, called by Gouverneur Morris "the germ of American Freedom," William Alexander and William Smith (Y. 1719), the first Yale lawyer in New York and the first Yale graduate from New York, were of counsel for the defense.   Though disbarred from speaking because they had attacked the validity of the Court, they found in Andrew Hamilton a fearless spokesman of their case against the arbitrary aggressions of Governor Cosby.   But Hamilton was only continuing, upon their suggestions, the fight which they had begun two or three years before in another case, and Smith himself had later been heard before the Assembly, contending for "the American doctrine of home rule, which found its ultimate expression in the declaration of 1776."—In 1763 there was a contest before the Connecticut Assembly as to the right of that body to interfere in the management of the College.   The presiding officers of both houses, and one-half of the members of the Upper House and one-sixth of the members of the Lower House were Yale graduates, and the counsel were Thomas Clap, the President of the College, who successfully argued against the right of interference, and on the other side Jared Ingersoll (Y. 1742) and William Samuel Johnson (Y. 1744). President Clap's victory seems to have settled the question forever.—The work of Yale men in the Constitutional Convention, in Congress, and in State Legislatures, seems to belong to another part of this work. But it is hard to refrain from noting that William Samuel Johnson (Y. 1744) and Oliver Ellsworth, who was a student at Yale for three years, drew the act of 1789 for the organization and regulation of the Federal Courts.—In the Dartmouth College case the thoughts of Jeremiah Mason (Y. 1788) formed in part the basis of Webster's famous argument in the Supreme Court—Jeremiah Mason, whom Webster ranked as the equal of Chief Justice Marshall and whose simplicity and directness of speech were, according to Mr. Lodge, largely accountable for Webster's perfection of "a style unsurpassed in modern oratory."—In 1860 in the Court of Appeals of New York the Lemmon slave case was heard—substantially a contest between the North and the South upon that slavery question which soon led to the Civil War. Charles O'Conor argued for the Virginian slave owner, and was successfully opposed by William M. Evarts (Y. 1837).—In the impeachment of Andrew Johnson in 1868, Evarts was again conspicuous, as leading counsel for the President, contending against a view which would make of the President a mere employee bound to do the bidding of the Congress, instead of a coördinate part of a well-balanced government.—In the Geneva Tribunal, Evarts again and his classmate Morrison T. Waite (afterwards Chief Justice) were counsel for our government in the first international dispute of large import and much difficulty settled by arbitration.

These instances must suffice to show that Yale has a right to be proud of the work of its alumni in the field of advocacy. And yet doubtless a greater aggregate contribution to the development of the law has been made by the host of Yale lawyers who, in inconspicuous ways, have been doing their work all over the land, backed by Yale training and the Yale character.

YALE IN EDUCATION

By

GEORGE E. VINCENT

Colonial Yale offered an education suited to the needs of the times. The curriculum of Greek, Latin, and Hebrew, mathematics, physics, logic, rhetoric, ethics, metaphysics, together with the serious practice of debating and declamation afforded admirable training for the graduates, a majority of whom were ministers and lawyers, sent out by Yale to be leaders in Southern New England. In a very real sense this was vocational education, and conscious preparation for public service. It is worth noting that it was a Yale man, Jared Eliot, who in these early days urged the application of science to agriculture.

Not until the beginning of the last century did changing conditions force upon the colleges new studies and methods. Yale was among the first to recognize the new needs. Political economy was added in 1824. Chemistry, geology, and botany had appeared in the curriculum even earlier. Benjamin Silliman's chemical laboratory became a recognized center of research and teaching. The Romance languages and, later, German were given a place. Thanks chiefly to the influence of Theodore Dwight Woolsey, political science and history were emphasized. Metaphysics developed into philosophy and psychology. Philology and English literature gradually gained academic standing. Of late all the social sciences, "the new humanities," have developed rapidly both on the side of theory, and in application to practical problems.

Perhaps Yale's greatest service to education in the last century was the impetus given to scientific studies and technical training by the establishment of the Sheffield Scientific School. While the classical courses admitted, a little grudgingly, a modest minimum of scientific studies, they refused to make room for the diversified and specialized pursuits which developed so rapidly after the middle of the nineteenth century. The Sheffield Scientific School met the new demand and gave Yale a place in the van of the modern movement. The influence of "Sheff" upon the subsequent development of the entire University has been significant.

Yale is a University not because it has certain professional schools in addition to its undergraduate colleges, but by virtue of the spirit of scholarship and investigation which dominates the advanced work of the institution. As early as 1847 Theodore Dwight Woolsey, on his return from study in Germany, introduced certain advanced or post-graduate courses—the first of the kind in this country. From that time on Yale has maintained and steadily developed graduate work in many fields, in several of which she has attained a position of eminence.

Around Yale College and the Sheffield Scientific School has grown up a group of professional schools in which the University has reason to feel increasing pride. The Law School gains steadily in standards and status. The Forest School, on a graduate basis, is recognized as the leader in this field. The Medical School, for a long time sadly hampered by lack of funds, is now on the eve of a new era of growth and accomplishment. The School of the Fine Arts has given Yale a distinction which has been enhanced by the notable success of the School of Music. The School of Religion expresses in a unique way Colonial Yale's spiritual earnestness reinterpreted to meet twentieth century needs.

Yale has been on the whole conservative. She has generally been content to let others make experiments in education. Yet she has not always followed. In certain things she has led. Thus Yale was the first explicitly to avow a purpose to train youth for public service, to introduce competitive scholarships, to promote scientific agriculture, to establish the degree of Doctor of Philosophy, to introduce in the Academic college the system of faculty government, to provide for the election of certain Fellows by

Alumni vote, to inaugurate the group system of studies, to begin the formal teaching of new branches of science, as for example, physiological chemistry, to establish new types of schools such as those of Fine Arts and Forestry.

Yale has exerted wide influence upon American education. She has provided the first presidents for eighteen colleges and universities, from Princeton in 1747 to the University of Chicago in 1891. One hundred and fifty-seven graduates of Yale have served as presidents of American institutions of higher education. Yale men have been leaders in Indian Education, in training for the Deaf and Dumb, in establishing Agricultural Experiment Stations, in founding the U. S. Geological Survey, in promoting higher education for women, in developing the United States Department of Education, in introducing European standards of Medical Education, and in founding a new type of institution in China. Among the notable leaders of American Education are such Yale men as Thomas H. Gallaudet, F. A. P. Barnard, Henry Barnard, Daniel C. Gilman, William T. Harris, Andrew D. White, and William R. Harper.

Yale's physical resources for educational work have during recent years developed rapidly. The newer laboratories and lecture halls are of the best type. In scientific apparatus, museum collections, and mechanical equipment the University ranks high. The library of an educational institution is a significant index of academic and scientific standing. Yale's collection of books, amounting to more than a million volumes, is one of the two largest owned by an American University.

The influence of an educational center is to be measured in terms of its spirit, ideals, instruction, and its contributions to new knowledge. In the field of research Yale has won honorable distinction. The names of Silliman, Olmsted, Gibbs, Dana, Marsh, Whitney, Sumner, are only the more conspicuous among scores which will be remembered in connection with the development of American scholarship. In literature Yale men have played an honorable part. The Yale Press and the *Yale Review* are worthy expressions of scholarly and literary productivity in New Haven.

Yale together with other American institutions of higher education is called to new duties. The Nation faces new tests and must rise to new levels of unity, power, and purpose. Industry and commerce grow more specialized and exacting, social problems are increasingly insistent, class cleavage is more obvious, governmental activities are multiplying, the world situation is forcing us to revise our traditional policies and shibboleths, to substitute a well-considered purpose for a fatuous faith in "manifest destiny." The power to think clearly, to feel soundly, to serve efficiently, will be needed as never before.

The educational ideals which arise from this situation are emerging; closer connection with the popular public high schools; specialized training for business, for diplomatic and consular service, for municipal and institutional positions, a broad-minded attitude toward public life; escape from the narrow prejudices of caste or section; a new sense of the meaning and possibilities of citizenship. No loyal son of Yale can doubt that his Alma Mater will continue to play a leading part in the new national life, and that New Haven will ever be a place, where in the quaint phrases of its first charter: "youth may be instructed in the Arts and Sciences, who through the blessing of Almighty God may be fitted for public employment, both in church and civil state."

YALE IN PUBLIC LIFE

By

HIRAM BINGHAM

When Yale was founded, the charter which the Connecticut ministers obtained from the Legislature of the Colony set forth the fact that *"several well-disposed and public-spirited persons . . . . have expressed by petition their earnest desires that full liberty and privilege be granted . . . . for the founding, suitably endowing and ordering a Collegiate School . . . . wherein youth may be instructed in the arts and sciences . . . .* [and] *fitted for public employment, both in church and civil state."* It was the evident intention of our founders that the sons of Yale should be prepared for public service. To some people this specific devotion to service for the state seems strange considering that the founders were Congregational ministers "robust in theology as became ministers of those days." We must admit, however, that they had clear vision and builded wisely.

Two hundred years later at the Bicentennial Celebration, Colonel Roosevelt, then President of the United States, himself a Harvard man, paid this tribute to the sons of Eli:—"I have never yet worked at a task worth doing, that I did not find myself working shoulder to shoulder with some son of Yale. I have never yet been in any struggle for righteousness or decency, that there were not men of Yale to aid me and give me strength and courage." The words of President Roosevelt were appreciated. Yale graduates have always taken pride in the number of their brothers who have been influential in the public life of the republic. We have had a President and Vice-President, more than a score of Cabinet Officers, three score Senators of the

United States, nearly three score Governors of states, and many members of Congress and of our diplomatic and consular service.

Even before the days of the republic, Yale men played a conspicuous part in public life. The record is a source of satisfaction and inspiration. Accordingly this seems an appropriate time to name some of the more distinguished among those who have toiled for the good of the state, although to speak of all who deserve mention would take far more space than is at my disposal. As has been truly said, "In every department of life in which faithful service has been rendered, some son of Yale has written his name near the summit." Let the roll, however abridged, be called in chronological order :—

In the Class of 1737 was Philip Livingston, destined to be a delegate to the Stamp Act Congress, Speaker of the Provincial Assembly and signer of the Declaration of Independence.—In 1741 graduated William Livingston, first Governor of New Jersey, who served in the first three sessions of the Continental Congress and continued in the public service until his death.—In the Class of 1744 we find William Samuel Johnson, who helped frame the Constitution of the United States. He too had been delegate to the Stamp Act Congress and represented his state in England as special agent. He was the first United States Senator from Connecticut.—In 1746 comes Lewis Morris, a signer of the Declaration of Independence.—In the class below him were two other students destined to be signers of the Declaration of Independence—namely, Oliver Wolcott, Governor of his state, active in the Continental Congress, and performing services of great public importance during the Revolution; and Lyman Hall, member of the Continental Congress and Governor of Georgia.—In 1758 was Silas Deane, who became a member of the Connecticut General Assembly and of the first two Continental Congresses; one of the leaders in the Preparedness movement of his day. We are told that without the supplies which he obtained, the victory of Saratoga would have been impossible. He later served his country as Ambassador to France.—In the Class of 1765 we find Manasseh Cutler, who secured the passage by Congress of the famous Ordinance of 1787 and served for years in the Massachusetts Legislature and in Congress. His classmate Theodore Sedgwick was a member of the Continental Congress and Speaker of the National House of Representatives.—In 1772 there is Abraham Baldwin, one of the framers of the United States Constitution and later United States Senator; in 1778 another Oliver Wolcott, one of our first Secretaries of the Treasury and later Governor of his state for ten years; and in 1781 Chancellor Kent, Chief Justice of the Supreme Court of New York state. Every member of the Bar knows of his celebrated editions and Commentaries.—In the Class of 1804 we find John Caldwell Calhoun, one of our most famous public servants. His long, brilliant career in Washington secures for him high rank in the list of those who have served Yale by serving America.—Yale has not sent many Governors to Massachusetts, but in the Class of 1812 was one of her best— "Honest John" Davis—whose career in Congress and as Governor was noted for practical sagacity and spotless integrity.— In 1815 we find John Middleton Clayton, conspicuous in the field of diplomacy; in 1833 Alphonso Taft, Secretary of War, Attorney General, and diplomat; in 1837 Samuel Jones Tilden, a national figure in political reform, Governor of New York and Democratic candidate for the presidency; and also William M. Evarts, Attorney General, Secretary of State, Senator; in 1846 Joseph Emerson Brown, Governor of Georgia, Chief Justice of that state, and United States Senator; and in 1847 Benjamin G. Brown, Senator, candidate for Vice President on the ticket with Horace Greeley.—The Class of 1853 had four distinguished men who spent their lives in public service: Senator Randall Lee Gibson, Attorney General Wayne MacVeagh, Justice George Shiras, and Ambassador Andrew D. White.

The number of Yale men who have gone into public life during the past sixty years is so great that we must leave most of them for the historian of the future to record. The names which will most readily occur to everyone are those of Justice Brewer, '56; Senator Depew, '56; Commissioner of Education William

T. Harris, '58; Simeon E. Baldwin, '61, Chief Justice and Governor of Connecticut; and William Howard Taft, '78, whose services as Governor of the Philippines, Secretary of War, and President of the United States mark him as the most distinguished man that Yale has sent into public life. The list might readily be prolonged, but enough has been said to show that the founders of Yale, were they with us to-day, would not be disappointed in their "collegiate school" which was to fit men "for public employment in civil state."

In conclusion, I can find no better words to express our hopes than these, used by the late Justice Brewer in the commemorative oration delivered at the Bicentennial:—"To-day the great temple of popular government in this Republic rises before the world the most magnificent structure on the political horizon. Her foundations rest on rocks more solid than New England granite; her architecture filled with a beauty richer than can be found in all the luxuriant growth of southern foliage and flower, and gilded with a shining splendor surpassing aught ever seen in California's golden sands; and in and upon all that lofty structure, from lowest wall to highest spire, Yale has written these immortal words: 'I train for public service.'"

YALE IN LITERATURE

By

WILLIAM LYON PHELPS

American literature is so poor in comparison with the literatures of Greece, Rome, England, France, Germany, Italy, and other countries, that I may be forgiven if I do not "point with pride" to Yale's exhibit. It is unfortunately true that no first-class creative writer has ever been graduated from Yale; but the same remark is equally descriptive of nearly all American institutions of learning. American universities are so much more numerous than American men of letters that there are not enough poets and novelists to "go around." I am using the word "writer" in the strictest sense; if I included theological and political thinkers, one would immediately name Jonathan Edwards and John C. Calhoun, and Yale would make a brave showing. Our university, as Mr. Stedman remarked, has always cultivated strength rather than grace; her ideal has been public service in war, in politics, in social betterment, and in science rather than in literary art. Yet she has sometimes been the first to bestow academic distinction upon great writers who were self-made. Yale was the first college to give a degree to Benjamin Franklin, to Mark Twain, and to James Whitcomb Riley.

It is also true that in the latter part of the eighteenth century Yale was a center of literary influence, and the "Hartford Wits," according to Professor Wendell of Harvard, ought to be placed to our credit. "At the time when the Hartford Wits wrote," said he, "no Harvard man had produced literature half so good as theirs." John Trumbull, of the class of 1767, was a distin-

JAMES FENIMORE COOPER
Class of 1806

guished poet and satirist; and President Timothy Dwight wrote
a great hymn, which will last as long as hymns are sung.

Fenimore Cooper is the only author of permanent and international fame connected with Yale, and the Faculty expelled
him for insubordination midway in his college course. It is my
earnest hope that some day his statue will adorn our campus,
for he really belongs to us. Through the generosity of the Class
of 1879, we have his portrait in oils, and the best biography of
him was written by Professor Lounsbury. E. C. Stedman, poet
and critic, was also disciplined by the Faculty, and years later
invited to a chair. His constant loyalty and devotion to Yale
remind one of James Russell Lowell, who was forbidden by the
Harvard Faculty to read his class poem, and responded in 1865
by reading the Commemoration Ode, the greatest poem produced
by the Civil War.

In the nineteenth century, there are some names of eminence
that it is safe to say can never be omitted from any comprehensive
"History of American Literature." These are N. P. Willis, '27,
whose *Life* by Professor Beers is more than worthy of the
subject; Donald G. Mitchell, '41, who attained fame early in
life with the *Reveries of a Bachelor,* and was both in mind
and character a perfect illustration of the finer qualities that
ought always to be associated with men of letters; E. R. Sill,
'61, some of whose poems are quoted somewhere in America
every day; F. M. Finch, '49, whose name was prophetic, for he
sang two songs that will not be forgotten, a stanza from one
of them being engraved on the floor of Memorial Hall; Henry A.
Beers, '69, a poet and story-writer, of whom the only justly
adverse comment can be, that he ought to have written more.

Yale's greatness as the mother of authors lies in the future.
A large number of young alumni in the twentieth century are
producing novels, short stories, plays, and poems in profusion.
The late Justus Miles Forman, '98, who was lost on the Lusitania,
had a long list of excellent works of fiction to his credit; Gouverneur Morris of the same class is at this moment a popular author;
so is Owen Johnson, 1900; Rupert Hughes, who took his M.A.

in course in 1899, has attained a wide reputation both as novelist and playwright; and in May, 1916, three new novels appeared from three recent graduates, which are notable for their display of potential powers. On one shelf in my library stand eighteen works of fiction, all written by living Yale graduates; and these constitute only a small fraction of the total literary production. In creative poetry, Brian Hooker, 1902, has won a place for himself among contemporary writers, and would be thought of immediately in any enumeration of living American poets; the same statement applies with equal truth and emphasis to W. R. Benét, 1907 S.

No sketch of Yale's contributions to literature should omit mention of the *Yale Literary Magazine,* which celebrates this year its eightieth birthday. This is the oldest monthly magazine—in or out of college circles—in America, and its standards were never higher than at the present moment.

One of the best things that has ever happened in the history of Yale's literary activities, was the founding, in 1911, of the *Yale Review,* under the able editorship of Wilbur L. Cross, then Professor of English in the Sheffield Scientific School, and now Dean of the Graduate School. Within five years, this periodical has reached an undisputed place in the front rank of American reviews, and is a fine illustration of, and at the same time, a sharp stimulus to the intellectual life of the University. Together with the recently founded Yale University Press, these two agencies have added immensely to the international fame of Yale. If every alumnus were a subscriber to the *Yale Review,* the university and the alumni would come together closer than ever before; and the alumni would more fully realise some of the highest purposes and some of the finest achievements of Yale, as a center of art and thought.

YALE IN JOURNALISM

By

NORRIS G. OSBORN

Yale in Journalism is a very large order even for one who has knocked about in it for approaching forty years, and has inevitably, in consequence, come into intimate contact with Yale men on the journalistic rush line. The Fourth Estate closely resembles the other three estates in that it blocks one's study of its personnel by hiding back of the lofty peaks the hosts below—men of far reaching achievement—who stretch from the fertile valleys up through the winding passes and jutting crags until the top is reached. If Yale could claim as members of her brotherhood Dana of the *New York Sun,* Greeley of the *New York Tribune,* Raymond of the *New York Times,* the elder Bowles of the *Springfield Republican,* and the sole picturesque survivor of the school of personal journalism, Watterson of the *Louisville Courier-Journal*—men whose careers have enriched the history of American journalism and stimulated it—they would be the first to renounce the exclusive distinction which popular fancy and fawning historians have conferred upon them. They would insist that they should not be crowned until a corresponding recognition had been conferred upon the subordinate officers and men in the journalistic trenches who, in a large degree, fitted their heads to the crowns they were so modestly to wear. In each of these newspaper offices, in all of them to-day, in fact in all commanding newspaper offices to-day, were and are expert craftsmen who won their degrees in the arts and sciences at Yale. If it were within the limits of good taste to poke about the ink-stained offices of newspapers being edited and printed to-day in the state from which Yale draws her chartered rights, I could write of men in whom the capacity to serve their communities is large, and whose devotion to the ideals absorbed at their Alma Mater radiates over a larger area than Connecticut herself possesses. Sufficient that the clerical members of the Corporation have invaded a Yale-edited newspaper for a life Fellow, and that the Alumni have done likewise in selecting one of their representatives on that body.

Not content with her own finished product, Yale reached out and brought into her brotherhood of journalists by means of honorary degrees Benjamin Franklin in 1753, the journal of whose origin is alive and one of the prosperous investments of the country. Henry C. Bunner was another adopted son of Yale whose editorial comments in *Puck* were in wisdom and courage fully paralleled by the sweetness of his verse and the calm of his philosophy. Whitelaw Reid of the *Tribune* was another. He rose to the chief editorship of that newspaper and then flew above the heights of the famous "Trib" tower and entered the most exclusive regions of political life. John Hay, whose practical newspaper apprenticeship the more fully equipped him for the gentle art of poesy, on the one hand, and the gracious science of diplomacy, on the other hand, dignified the list. Dashing General "Joe" Hawley of the *Hartford Courant* was, in his turn, shown the way into the inner sanctum of Yale Associations.

Among those "Made at Yale" none wrote himself more blessedly upon the life of the state of Connecticut than Horace Bushnell, '27, who, upon graduation, entered the employ of the *New York Journal of Commerce,* finally abandoning the pen of the journalist for the pen of the preacher. Edward C. Stedman, '53, the banker-poet, supplemented his training at Yale with a course on the staff of the *New York Evening Post.* No more stalwart knight of the pen, the paste pot, and the scissors than Ellis H. Roberts, '50, was ever given the blessing of his Alma Mater. The famous class of '53, in addition to Stedman, gave to the profession notable journalists in the persons of George W. Smalley, long the London correspondent of the *New York Tribune* and later the New York correspondent of the *London Times,* and

Isaac H. Bromley who can be claimed by the *Norwich Bulletin,* the *Hartford Post* and the *New York Tribune.* Unlike in method and temperament, these two men rank among the very highest in the history of American journalism; the former severe and searching in his presentation and analysis of current events, the latter incisive and satirical in his consideration of men and measures. It was Bromley who inquired of an indignant candidate for political office, whose pretensions he had ridiculed and whose chances of success he ruined: "What did you plant yourself in front of my gun for?" William Parsons, '68, who passed a stormy career as the editor of the *New Haven Register* for a few years, and later as the editor of the *Hartford Telegram,* gave heavy weight championship blows and reeled not when they were returned. Clarence Deming, '72, as a member of the staff of the *New York Evening Post,* later as the editor of the *New Haven Morning News* and still later as a general correspondent, was the personification of the ardent reformer in a varied field of journalism. The Elliot brothers, Charles S., '67, and Henry R., '71, gave influential service to the *New Haven Morning Journal-Courier* and elsewhere.

The field of investigation and classification could be widely extended if there were records to which one could turn, or if I felt warranted in recalling the many—fearless and progressive lancers—who are at this moment battling at the journalistic Armageddon for the Lord of incorruptible journalism without fear or favor. But as I leave them at their desks, at headquarters, or in the field, the following, who have crossed the great divide, were men who hit hard for the welfare of society and the overthrow of the spineless and the vicious, and belong therefor in Yale's hall of journalistic fame: Abner L. Train, '53, William E. Foster, '60, Walter Allen, '63, Samuel A. York, '63, Charles H. Adams, '66, William A. McKinney, '68, E. P. Clark, '70, and John Addison Porter, '78.

It was in 1900 that the widow of "Ike" Bromley, '53, gave the University the sum of $5,000 for a lectureship in loving memory of her husband. The deed of gift reveals the understanding the donor had of her husband's inner consciousness. It provided that lectures on journalism should be arranged as often as once in four years; the University authorities being otherwise given a wide latitude in their choice of subjects, provided only they had to do with literature or public affairs. Could he have expressed a wish, he would have arranged the gift thus, anxious, on the one hand, that all Yale men should receive a first-hand knowledge of journalism, without, on the other hand, surfeiting them with a too frequent treatment of it. Two Yale men have appeared in the course with the authority of distinguished journalistic service, Charles Hopkins Clark, '71, editor of the *Hartford Courant* and Hart Lyman, '73, until recently, and for many years, editor of the *New York Tribune*. Among others, not Yale men, who have lectured in this course are St. Clair McKelway, formerly editor of the *Brooklyn Eagle,* A. Maurice Low, the publicist, Talcott Williams of the Columbia School of Journalism, and Bliss Perry, editor and essayist.

I by no manner of means regard this as a sufficient survey of Yale in Journalism. It will, however, answer a purpose if it leads another, better equipped, to do justice to a group of Yale men who have done their full share to carry into the life of their country the Yale Spirit.

YALE'S PERIODICALS

By

WILBUR LUCIUS CROSS

———

Yale has many periodicals. Of those conducted by the under-graduates, the oldest is *The Yale Literary Magazine,* which was established in 1836. Its first editors set a high standard of literary excellence which has been well maintained through nearly a century. In its earlier history, its pages were illumined by William M. Evarts, Andrew D. White, D. G. Mitchell, D. C. Gilman, and T. R. Lounsbury. To win the *Lit.* board is still an undergraduate honor of the first rank. As the College expanded, *The Yale Courant* (1867) and *The Yale Record* (1872) came into being to deal more intimately with the life of the Campus. During the half century of their existence, they have undergone many changes. They are now illustrated maga-zines, written in a light or humorous vein. Once issued every week, *The Record* is now a fortnightly, and *The Courant* a monthly. *The Yale Sheffield Monthly* (founded in 1894 as *The Yale Scientific Monthly*) is a flourishing organ of the undergraduate body in the Sheffield Scientific School. Likewise the Yale Law School has its own organ in *The Yale Law Journal,* which was founded in 1891. Its editorial board is selected by the law faculty from the students on the basis of scholarship and editorial capacity. Among its contributors are many of the leading jurists of the country. *The Yale Daily News,* which made its appearance as a little sheet in 1878, has become a fearless exponent of undergraduate opinion on all subjects affecting the interests of students in Yale College and the Sheffield Scientific School. The chairman of its editorial board wields an immense influence.

The publication most closely in touch with the graduates is *The Alumni Weekly,* which began in 1891 as a sort of *Yale News,* to be issued weekly for the benefit of the alumni; but under the editorship of Mr. Lewis S. Welch and Mr. Edwin Oviatt, it has developed into a magazine for the discussion of those larger problems which always confront a university, and press for solution. Just a century ago there was established in New Haven a magazine called *The Christian Spectator,* which was succeeded in 1843 by *The New Englander.* These once influential magazines are the direct progenitors of *The Yale Review,* which, after passing through the phase of an economic journal conducted by Professor Henry W. Farnam, was converted five years ago into a quarterly for the publication of articles in the domain of public affairs, art, science, and literature. The writer of this article assumed the editorship with Professors Edward B. Reed and Henry S. Canby as able assistants. Though edited by men on the Yale faculty and bearing the Yale name, this magazine is not an official organ of the University, nor does it ever discuss the educational and administrative policies of the University. It aims to address those readers everywhere who are desirous of keeping abreast with the thought and literature of the times as presented by the ablest writers. *The Yale Review* is an American magazine, national in scope and character.

Of Yale's periodicals devoted to research in special fields, the pioneer is *The American Journal of Science,* which, established by Benjamin Silliman in 1818, has had a long and most distinguished career. For many years it was edited by Professor James D. Dana, the geologist, who was succeeded by his son, Professor Edward S. Dana, the present editor. Throughout its history, it has had on its board as associates other scientific men of the first rank, such as Dr. Asa Gray and Professor Louis Agassiz. *The American Journal of Science,* more than any other periodical published in the United States, has been a record of the great scientific discoveries of the last century. Several of its contributors have been among the most active members of "The Connecticut Academy of Arts and Sciences" (established in 1799), in the transactions of which first appeared the epoch-making papers on mathematical physics by Josiah Willard Gibbs.

Professor John D. Irving of the Sheffield faculty is the editor-in-chief of *The Journal of Economic Geology,* dating from 1905. This periodical deals with the commercial side of geological work such as the origin of ore deposits, their occurrence, and classification. It is the only publication of the kind in the English language. Similarly, Professor Ross G. Harrison is the managing-editor of *The Journal of Experimental Zoology,* established in 1904 to provide a place for the publication of investigations in experimental zoology. Within the short period of its existence, it has gained an international reputation. Professor Lafayette B. Mendel of the Sheffield Scientific School is one of the editors of *The Journal of Biological Chemistry,* published by the Rockefeller Institute for Medical Research. Likewise Professor Percey F. Smith is one of the three editors of *The Transactions of the American Mathematical Society.* Yale is also represented on the editorial boards of various other periodicals in science, history, and law. Finally, the American Oriental Society, founded in 1845, has always been definitely associated with Yale, though its first meetings were held in Boston. The late Professor Edward E. Salisbury was in the early years of its existence "its life and soul." He had a great successor in Professor William D. Whitney, who was for a long period the chief editor of its organ known as *The Journal of the American Oriental Society.* Of late years its responsible editors have been Professors Hopkins, Oertel, and Torrey, of the Yale faculty. Throughout its history, the *Journal* has been truly representative of Oriental learning in the United States. The contributions of Professor Whitney gave it European fame.

THE YALE UNIVERSITY PRESS

By

GEORGE PARMLY DAY

The Yale University Press was founded in 1908 with the ideal of striving to advance the cause of scholarship and letters throughout the world by the publication of works possessing permanent interest and value, whether or not the authors were connected with Yale. It therefore differed at the very outset from somewhat similar enterprises previously established in other American universities, where the emphasis had been placed more upon the immediate service which could be rendered by a press to its own university through the printing of its catalogues and other pamphlets and the publication of works by members of its faculty, and of magazines, theses, etc., written by its students. In its operations the Yale University Press has, of course, sought to advance the interests of the university whose name it bears, and to enhance its reputation as an institution where research shall receive the proper reward of prompt recognition and adequate publication of the results achieved. It has not failed to keep in mind the undoubted influence of the publishing activities of a university in attracting to the service of that university, and subsequently retaining in its service, men doing original work in various fields. The Press has been eager also to further the early promotion of younger teachers at Yale through the publication of their works. It has recognized the fact that general publishing houses, under the necessity of avoiding annual deficits and of paying dividends to their stockholders, cannot as a rule risk bringing out a certain type of book unless guaranteed a substantial part of its cost. The Press has felt, however, that it must stand ready to publish works like *The Records of the Federal*

Convention of 1787 and *The Meaning of God in Human Experience,* even if no subsidy be guaranteed and the risk be great, as otherwise it would not be carrying out its announced purpose. But while constantly seeking to be of all the service it should thus be to its home community, the Yale University Press has endeavored also never to lose sight of the fact that it could not fulfill its true function except by making such service to Yale merely a part of its work for the whole world of letters.

As to how successful the Press has been in living up to this ideal, critics can best judge, perhaps, each for himself, after a perusal of its catalogue; or, better still, of the books described therein. In the latest edition of this there are listed about two hundred works, exclusive of the many titles in the series of *Yale Studies in English,* the *Transactions of the Connecticut Academy of Arts and Sciences,* and the *Cornell Studies in English,* all of which are now issued under the Yale imprint. Of this total of two hundred books, over one-half have been written by others than members of the Yale Faculty. Naturally the volumes of addresses delivered by lecturers invited to speak at the University account in part for this. Even if such lectures be excluded, however, it will be found that about one-third of the publications of the Yale University Press are by authors not officially connected with Yale, and that over one-half of these are by men actively associated in the work of other universities here and abroad.

In the selection of works to be published under its imprint, the Press has enjoyed the coöperation of many within the University and outside working through the Council's Committee on Publications of Yale University, without whose sanction no volume can be issued by the Press. It has been significant of the Committee's appreciation of the responsibility placed upon it that it has symphathized with the proper feeling of the Press that no manuscript should be rejected merely because of prejudice against the subject chosen by the author or disagreement with the views expressed by him—provided his work has been written with the ability and accuracy desirable in a volume to be issued under the auspices of the University. In other words the Committee has not construed its function to be the limiting of the activities of the Press, but has helped to increase these: endorsing promptly, for example, the policy adopted at an early date by the Press of not confining itself to the publication of scientific works, text books, and theses, but of broadening its field by including a large number of volumes of very general interest.   Through its adherence to this policy, it may be said in passing, the Yale University Press has done more than win for itself an enviable position in the book trade and with the reading public.   For it has, in the opinion of librarians, book-sellers, and those in charge of the publishing activities of other institutions, helped other university presses by removing in large part a certain popular prejudice against these, based on the idea that they were formed to publish only those works which the average man would never read.

In the distribution of the books published by it, the Yale University Press shortly after its organization obtained the coöperation of the Oxford University Press, London, as its foreign representative, and the majority of its publications now bear the joint imprint of Oxford and Yale.   During the past year the Press has taken an active part in the formation in this country of the University Press Association, which it is hoped will ultimately include the leading American university presses and prove of advantage to all through coöperative distribution of their works.

In the financing of its increasing business the Yale University Press has relied upon the assistance of many friends who have realized not only the value of the service rendered by it but also the impossibility of its doing its best work except at a financial loss, in spite of the fact that its officers and trustees have served without salary and that it has never paid dividends or interest on the working capital advanced to it.   The total of gifts made to the University for the benefit of the Press up to June 30, 1916, was $46,750: of which sum $33,150, in accordance with the wishes of the donors, has been advanced to the Press for use as working capital; while the balance of $13,600 represents its only permanent general endowment.   In addition to these gifts, however, the University has received a number of publication funds to further work in certain fields: the largest being the foundation established in 1914 by the gift of twenty thousand dollars by the Kingsley Trust Association (Scroll and Key Society of Yale College) to enable the Department of History to carry on its already notable series of publications. A number of other organizations, such as the Connecticut Academy of Arts and Sciences, the Elizabethan Club, the Dramatic Association, the *Yale Daily News,* and the *Banner and Pot Pourri,* have seen, in furthering the work of the Press, an unusual opportunity to serve the University, and have, as have some of the graduates, made gifts from time to time to assist the publication of various works. Other permanent foundations include that established by the late John E. Parsons and those given in memory of Henry Weldon Barnes, '82, Mary Stevens Hammond, Frederick John Kingsbury, '46, Alexander Kohut, Herbert Adolph Scheftel, '98, and William Chauncey Williams, '22 M.S., and William Cook Williams, '50 M.S. With the continued increase in such publication funds, which seems as probable as it is desirable, should come not only an expansion of the work of the corporation known as the Yale University Press but also, through this, an increased activity in many educational departments of the University itself. Many signs of this are already apparent: in the starting, for example, of the *Yale Oriental Series,* modelled on the lines of the Historical Series mentioned; in the announcement of publications planned by the School of Law; in the beginning of publications under the auspices of the School of the Fine Arts; and in the gift of the Williams Memorial Fund to assist publications in the field of medicine. It is by such publications that Yale University can, in the words of Sir William Osler, do "university extension work of the finest character." It is by having made possible this work for Yale and by the assistance it has rendered to scholars there and elsewhere that the Yale University Press may fairly be said to have demonstrated its right to continued existence and to have earned the endowment which it has needed from the outset, but which it could not secure as long as its work was regarded by many as an experiment and its vision of its destiny as a dream.

THE YALE LIBRARY

By

ADDISON VAN NAME

Each Member brought a Number of Books and presented them to the Body; and laying them on the Table, said these Words, or to this Effect; *"I give these Books for the founding a College in this Colony."* Clap, *Annals,* p. 3.

These few books and fewer words, which automatically set the College in motion, form as a matter of course the prologue to any story of the Library. At Cambridge, some years earlier, books had played a part in a similar but not quite parallel transaction; for it took all of John Harvard's two hundred and sixty volumes and the half of his estate besides to start Harvard College. Neither there nor here would Carlyle's famous dictum—"The true University of these days is a Collection of Books"—have found acceptance, but that books were the proper foundation there seems to have been, here at least, no manner of doubt.

The first considerable gift toward the upbuilding of the Library was a collection of seven hundred volumes sent over in 1714 by Jeremiah Dummer, agent of the Connecticut Colony in London. On the list of donors, still in the Library, are many distinguished names, headed by Sir Richard Steele, who sent "All the Tatlers and Spectators, being eleven volumes in Royal paper, neatly bound and gilt." Sir Isaac Newton gave his *Principia* and *Optics,* and the Greek *Thesaurus* of Stephanus, in four volumes folio, all of which, with the exception of the *Optics,* are still here. Dummer, by whose active interest the books had been obtained, himself contributed ninety-two, and Governor Yale added forty, an earnest of the larger gifts to follow.

When the change of base to New Haven was executed in 1716, in the face of bitter opposition from Saybrook, the books which made up certainly the chief part, and possibly the whole, of the *impedimenta* which the "Collegiate School" possessed were prudently left behind. They reached New Haven two years later, only after a struggle in which about 250 of the most valuable books were lost. In number at least the loss was made good by a box of books lately arrived from Governor Yale.

The most important event in the Library history of the first hundred years was Bishop Berkeley's gift of 900 volumes in 1733, pronounced by Rector Clap "the finest collection of books that ever came together at one time into America," and judged by him to have cost at least £400 sterling. In the appendix (dated 1765) to the *Annals* he says: "We have a good Library, consisting of about 4,000 volumes, well furnished with ancient authors, such as the Fathers, Historians and Classicks, many modern valuable books of Divinity, History, Philosophy, and Mathematicks, but not many authors who have wrote within these thirty years," i. e. since the date of the Berkeley gift, after which time little of value could have come to the Library either by gift or purchase. Between the total here given (4,000), and that of his *Catalogue* printed in 1755 (3,000), we do not hesitate to choose the latter, which agrees with the pre-Revolutionary estimate of President Stiles. During the Revolution the greater part of the books were removed to Northford, Durham, and Watertown, out of the way of the enemy, with the usual result of such removes. When brought back in 1782 the number in the Library was found to be 2,448. In 1791 it rose to 2,700, and in 1800 may have been 3,500. These and a Library fund which, starting with a gift of £10 from Rev. Jared Eliot in 1763, had now reached $1,237, were the net result of the century's growth.

The next twenty-five years but little more than doubled this accomplishment. At length, in the second quarter of the century, the upward movement definitely began. A gift of $5,000 to the Library fund in 1833, was followed in 1836 by another of $10,000, which is further noteworthy as the largest gift ever received by the College up to that time from any one person—Bishop Berkeley's Newport farm, valued at £3,000, and his books alone excepted. For forty years it remained the largest single contribution to the fund. More than this, the Library which—to speak in academic phrase—had entered "Yale College" as Freshman in 1718; the Athenaeum as Sophomore in 1763; the Lyceum as Junior in 1803; and the old Chapel as Senior in 1824, rooming in each case on the upper floor, was at length in 1843 admitted to the graduate department and came into possession of a dwelling of its own, the finest on the campus. The wings of the building were given to the Linonian and Brothers Libraries as a just return for their invaluable services. In 1850 they had each about 10,000 volumes and the College Library about 21,000, with a fund of $25,000, which for twenty years remained almost stationary. Then it rose step by step until in 1890, when Chittenden Hall was opened, it had reached $75,000, the books meantime increasing to 170,000. From that point the fund mounted rapidly, soaring rather than climbing, to its present level—$979,000—an average of $300,000 for each decade. About one-third is specifically a book fund and two-thirds a maintenance fund. The accessions to the Library, more than one-half of which have come from gifts and bequests, have for some years past exceeded 30,-000 volumes a year, and the total number of volumes now in the University Library is placed in the latest statement of the Librarian at about 850,000. To meet this great increase, Linsly Hall, erected in 1906 from the bequest of William B. Ross, Y. C. 1852, has hardly more than sufficed. Larger provision for a longer future remains to be made.

The value of a library has no direct relation to the number of volumes, but in the case of very large numbers the difficulties of just estimation of its worth increase greatly. Some idea, however, of the wealth and variety of the Yale Library may be had from even brief mention of a few of its more important special collections. These include the Edward E. Salisbury Oriental Collection of about 6,000 volumes and 90 Arabic manuscripts; the Count Landberg Arabic Manuscripts, 842 in number; the J. Sumner

Smith Russian Collection of over 6,000 volumes; the Count Riant Collection of Scandinavian History and Geography of 5,000 volumes; the Albert S. Wheeler Roman Law Collection of 5,000 volumes, with a fund of $18,000; the Henry S. Wagner English and Irish Political and Economic Tracts numbering 9,700; the Latin-American Collection of 41,000 volumes and much manuscript material, of which 15,000 volumes are devoted to Mexico and 11,000 to Peru; the Henry M. Dexter Collection of Congregational History and Polity of 1,850 volumes; the Owen F. Aldis Collection of American Literature of about 2,400 volumes, comprising first and important editions of American authors; the William A. Speck Goethe Collection, of which the "Faust" items alone number 1,200 volumes; and the William Loring Andrews Collection of Early Printed Books.

In addition to the central collection at the University Library there are upwards of thirty departmental and special Yale libraries with a total number of about 150,000 volumes and funds amounting to about $139,000. Notable among these are the Law Library of 40,000 volumes with a fund of $29,000 and the collections of the School of Religion, 33,000 volumes in all, with a fund of $83,000, including the George E. Day Mission Library of 12,000 volumes, which has not merely a maintenance fund of $77,000, but a building of its own. These, added to the number of books in the University Library itself (850,000 volumes), bring the total of all Yale libraries to 1,000,000 volumes, with library funds amounting to $1,100,000.

Although not an integral part of the University Library itself, the collections of the Elizabethan Club are too notable to be overlooked. The unusual group of Shakespeare quartos and folios from the Huth catalogue would alone be sufficient to give it distinction. Other rare sixteenth and seventeenth century English books and choice later editions add to its value and have already made it a center of promising literary activity.

Reminded anew of its first arrival in New Haven, with nothing on its back and little in its pocket, and of the long struggle through which it had to pass, the University Library takes occasion to

congratulate heartily the Free Public Library of New Haven, now
only thirty years old, on the work accomplished and the admirable
equipment it possesses.   Each has a field of its own, but there is
common ground where both can and should coöperate.   The City
Library has in building and fund not less than half a million of
dollars; the University Libraries, a million and a half.   Back of
these are the books, the sources and the accumulated stores of our
power.   In an eminent sense they are public utilities, and the City
of New Haven being nearest to the source receives the first
benefits.

YALE LEXICOGRAPHERS

By

MARIAN P. WHITNEY

It is due rather to a happy chance than to a fixed educational policy that Yale has been, since the founding of this Republic, the center of American lexicography, but no review of her intellectual influence on our nation and on the world can be complete which does not take into account the remarkable work done by her sons in this important field. For the three great dictionaries which, during almost one hundred years, have had the widest circulation among English speaking peoples, and which have most strongly influenced the speech and usage of our language, all owed their being to Yale men.

Noah Webster, the pioneer lexicographer of Yale and of the United States, did more than any other man to give his country that unity of language which has proved to be the most solid basis of our national unity. After graduating from Yale in 1778 he taught school for a time, and it was then that, "in order to combat the general inattention to the grammatical purity and elegance of our native language," he compiled the famous *Spelling-book,* which for more than three quarters of a century was studied by almost every American child. It has had a wider circulation in this country than any other book except the Bible, more than 71,000,000 copies having been sold. By this book Webster "contributed greatly to uniformity of pronunciation in the United States and . . . secured the general adoption of a simpler system of spelling than that current in England."

Webster's life-work was, however, his *American Dictionary of the English Language,* to which he devoted more than thirty years of labor. He brought to his work a natural love of words, their use and their meaning; a very real talent for concise and exact definition; an unusually wide experience as farmer, teacher, editor, lawyer, and pamphleteer; and a conviction that the work he was engaged upon was of the greatest importance to the future of his country. "As an independent nation," he says, "our honor requires us to have a system of our own in language as well as in government." Johnson's Dictionary, published in 1755, had been based on the authority of English literature and of the written word; Webster included in his not only the language of literature, but that of familiar daily life and of business. The spoken word was to him quite as interesting and important as the written; for him English was a living language, belonging alike to England and to America, and he gave equal weight to the usage of each country.

The first edition of his great quarto dictionary appeared in 1828, and contained 70,000 words, including "12,000 words and from 30,000 to 40,000 definitions which had not appeared in any earlier dictionary." Webster's dictionaries were the first to contain the historical and geographical statistics and other encyclopedic matter which have helped to make the dictionary a general book of reference in every household. From the point of view of the philologist Webster's first edition left much to be desired, but its publication was a great literary achievement for so young a nation. It met with speedy and most flattering success, not only in this country but in England. Later editions, prepared under the direction of distinguished philologists and with the coöperation of experts in every subject, many of whom have been found among the faculty and graduates of Yale, have enormously developed and enlarged the original work and supplied every early deficiency. But Webster himself has left his mark deeply on all succeeding dictionaries, for as Sir James Murray, editor of the *New English Dictionary,* says: "Webster was a great man, a born definer of words."

Joseph Worcester, the second of the sons of Yale to give his name to a great dictionary, was, like Webster, a country boy. He entered Yale in 1809, graduating in the Class of 1811. He,

NOAH WEBSTER
Class of 1778

too, began his career as a school teacher, and his first published works were school books. In 1828 he published his first lexicographical work, a new edition of Johnson, and in 1829 made an abridged edition of Webster's dictionary. He published his own first brief English dictionary in 1830, and after successive enlargements and additions he issued in 1860 his *Dictionary of the English Language,* containing the final fruits of his labors. Worcester is more conservative than Webster. He has a wider knowledge of language and of literature, due to the age in which he lived and to the advance of scholarship by which he profited. His main interest is for the literary rather than the colloquial language; he rejects many words which Webster included, and in disputed points goes back to the traditional usage. He first introduced illustrations into his dictionary and sought the help of able experts in the definition of technical terms. The sale of his work was very large both here and in England, and for many years "Webster" and "Worcester" were almost synonymous with the word dictionary.

The third dictionary "made at Yale" is not, like the two others, the life-work of its main editor, nor does it bear his name. In 1882 the time had passed when a dictionary could be a one-man affair. When Mr. Roswell-Smith, the president of the Century Company, conceived the idea of publishing a great dictionary on modern lines, full enough to supply every need of the general educated public, he turned for help to William Dwight Whitney, who had been for almost thirty years a member of the faculty of Yale and who was a philologist by profession, a student of language in its widest sense, and an acknowledged leader of American scholarship. The first plan of revising and enlarging a dictionary recently published in England was soon cast aside, and it was decided to make an entirely new dictionary which should embody the best features of all that had gone before, and to associate with it the name of the great publishing house which was ready to contribute to it unstintingly of its time, labor, and money. Professor Whitney was editor-in-chief and responsible for the whole work, but he had associated with him a large and competent staff of experts in all fields of knowledge, among them many Yale men. Whitney was, like Webster, a convinced spelling-reformer, and a believer in our language as a living thing, whose natural development should not be checked and hampered by too great respect for tradition. In deciding disputed points he considered modern usage as well as literary tradition, and was not afraid to put American usage on an equal footing with that of the mother country. In spite of the great size and cost of the *Century Dictionary,* more than 180,000 copies have been sold here and in England. On its publication in 1889 the *Nation* hailed it as "the handsomest dictionary that ever was made," "the Apotheosis of Webster," and some twenty years later the *Encyclopædia Britannica,* in speaking of the encyclopedic dictionary, said: "The most notable work of its class in English is the Century Dictionary. Next to the New English Dictionary it is the most complete and scholarly of English lexicons."

YALE IN SCIENCE

By

WILLIAM T. SEDGWICK

In 1716 science, as we think of it to-day, had no existence. Mathematics, having come down from the Greeks along with philosophy, art, and literature, held a high place in education; but science as a separate branch of learning or as an educational discipline was unknown. There were then no "scientists," but only physicians, mathematicians, and a very few nature philosophers. The word "science" was familiar enough, but when the poet Gray wrote in 1750 of that nameless youth "to fortune and to fame unknown" whom he has immortalized in the *Elegy,*—

Fair Science frown'd not on his humble birth—

he did not mean that physics, chemistry, and biology, or mathematics, astronomy, and engineering, had passed him by: he meant only that the young man was uneducated. Jared Eliot, of the Class of 1706, was a compound of physician and clergyman, a naturalist, and a philosophical farmer, but, despite Ben Franklin's praise of his stories "told with so much propriety and humor," and his pastor's tribute that "perhaps no man in his day has slept so little and done so much," we can hardly call him a scientist. Eliot came from Guilford, and we hear of no other like him for seventy years, until we reach David Bushnell, of Saybrook and the Class of 1775, originator of the submarine and the torpedo. But neither for Bushnell nor for Eli Whitney, of the Class of 1792, inventor of the cotton gin, can we claim the name of scientist in the modern sense.

At length, however, in the Class of 1796 comes one worthy to be called Yale's first, and for fifty years thereafter her foremost, man of science—the elder Silliman.   The scientific age was now at hand, if not actually begun.   Mathematics, with its cognate science, astronomy, had in recent centuries added to its ancient reputation, but with the physical and natural sciences it was different.   Physics was still "natural philosophy" and the biological sciences were still "natural history" when the nineteenth century began.   It was time that American colleges, even if remote and small and poor, should feel the thrill and awake to the new age already opening.   It is therefore interesting to learn from Secretary Stokes's invaluable *Memorials of Eminent Yale Men* that Natural Philosophy had been made part of the title of a Yale professorship in 1770, and had been effectively taught even earlier by President Clap, but practically without experiments (demonstrations) or laboratory tests (illustrations).   And in 1802, as if to meet the future half way, Benjamin Silliman, an agreeable and promising young tutor of twenty-three, was selected by President Dwight "for the newly established chair of chemistry and natural history."   But, like the beginning physicians of the olden time, Silliman was without experience in his new profession and had to get experience by practicing upon his patients.   To his credit be it said he went to Philadelphia, then the principal scientific center of America, there to study his profession for two winters.

Silliman proved to be one of the pioneers in American science, a great teacher, a wonderfully popular lecturer, and a beneficent influence throughout the whole country.   He did not do great original work in science, such as Willard Gibbs did a generation later, but he held high the new lamp of science in his day and generation and lighted the way for many who have come after him.   Benjamin Franklin, of Pennsylvania, and Benjamin Thompson (Count Rumford), of Massachusetts, had a worthy disciple in Benjamin Silliman, of Connecticut.   Silliman's undisputed position as the leading science teacher of his time is proved by his call in 1839 to give the first course of lectures for the opening of the new Lowell Institute in Boston.   His subject was "Geology" and his twelve lectures, as well as later courses on

"Chemistry," proved so popular that every course he gave had to be repeated. With one exception the elder Silliman has been heard more often at the Lowell Institute than any other lecturer in its whole history. His most conspicuous service to science was the establishment and maintenance of what was known for a whole generation as *Silliman's Journal,* now the *American Journal of Science,* to-day ably edited by his grandson, Professor Dana.

We must pass rapidly over many whose names and works have adorned the annals of Yale:—over physicians like Benjamin Gale and Nathan Smith; over geologists like Dana, Whitney, and King; over mathematical teachers like Loomis and Chauvenet; over the astronomers, such as Newton, the chemists such as Johnson, and the paleontologists such as Marsh:—to dwell for a moment upon the greatest scientist of all, Willard Gibbs, of the Class of 1858. Gibbs's place in Yale science is so commanding that of him we may say, as was said of the cup-winning yacht *America,* when it rushed across the line and Queen Victoria asked "Who is second?"—"Your Majesty, there is no second."

Willard Gibbs was essentially a mathematician and as such he ranks among the highest. But he is best known for his work in mathematical physics and in theoretical or physical chemistry. He was a quiet, almost a shy man—to most Yale men unknown even by name, and but scantily and tardily understood and appreciated, even by those who should have estimated him at his high value. Yet "except in his own country" he was and is honored beyond almost any American man of science. His *Studies in Thermodynamics* had the rare distinction of translation into German by the highest German authority, William Ostwald, and Gibbs's "Phase Rule" is one of the best known corner stones of modern chemistry. His biographer, Professor Bumstead, has said of him:—

Professor Gibbs worked alone in a field in which he had no rivals and no helpers. . . . Yet his very numerous results were correct, were of the highest importance, and were extremely general in their application. . . . Considered merely as an intellectual *tour de force,* there are very few chapters in the history of science which can be compared with this [his principal paper] ; as an example of scientific prediction it is probably without a rival in the number and complexity of the relations discovered, by *a priori* reasoning, in a science essentially experimental.

Yale's largest and best known contribution to the present scientific age has been her great school of pure and applied science,—the Sheffield Scientific School,—in 1847 tolerated rather than fostered as *The Yale Analytical Laboratory,* in the old president's house on College street; in 1854 formally considered a separate section of the recently established Graduate Department and entitled *The Yale Scientific School,* and awarded its present name in honor of Mr. Sheffield and his munificent gifts, in 1861. At the time, Mr. Sheffield's donation was voted by the Corporation "the most considerable benefaction which Yale College has received from any one man from its foundation." From this splendid School which now rivals in its number of students the much older Academical Department, and is likely, in an age ever increasingly scientific and industrial, soon to surpass it, more than five thousand graduates have been sent out into the world thoroughly equipped with the principles and conversant with the methods of science. From it has come also the "group system" of undergraduate studies, a system which by a kind of survival of the fittest seems likely before long to displace all others in American educational institutions. Best of all, enriched with the priceless example, the wisdom, and the vision, of the founders of the School—Brush, Brewer, Johnson, Norton, Porter, Lyman, and many more—and of their worthy successors, Chittenden, Hastings, Penfield, Osborne and their colleagues, as well as of eminent graduates not a few, the spirit of science here as in every department of Yale has always been of that lofty and noble quality attributed to our modern age by a distinguished son of Harvard and a theologian who says,—

A greater gain to the world than all the growth of scientific knowledge is the growth of the scientific spirit, with its courage and serenity, its disciplined conscience, its intellectual morality, its habitual response to any disclosure of the truth.

YALE INVENTIONS

I. THE SUBMARINE AND TORPEDO

(DAVID BUSHNELL, Class of 1775)

By

ROBERT W. NEESER

There is an entry in the acts of the Governor and Council of Safety of Connecticut, under date February 2, 1776, that "Mr. Bushnell, by request of the Governor and Council, appeared before them and gave an account of his machine for blowing up ships." This was none other than the terrible "Turtle" which David Bushnell of Saybrook, Connecticut, projected in his Freshman year at Yale, in 1771, and perfected about the time of his graduation from the College.

The external shape of the submarine vessel bore some resemblance to two upper tortoise shells floating in the water tail down. It was a little over seven feet long and six feet deep, large enough to hold the operator and sufficient air to last him half an hour. There was an ingenious water-gauge, a compass, an oar, formed on the principle of an old-fashioned screw, for propelling the vessel, and another oar which caused the vessel to sink or rise. There was also a ballast tank and a heavy lead keel which could be released in case of emergency. Behind the vessel, above the rudder, was attached a magazine containing one hundred and fifty pounds of powder which was fired by a percussion device, timed by means of clockwork. A rope extended from the magazine to a wood screw which the operator was expected to screw into the bottom planking of the enemy's ship before releasing the magazine for explosion.

Bushnell made many trials with the "Turtle" before attempting an attack against the British ships on the coast. "In the first essay with the submarine vessel," he wrote, "I took care to prove its strength to sustain the great pressure of the incumbent water, when sunk deep, before I trusted any person to descend much below the surface." Great difficulty was experienced in finding a skilful operator for the vessel. The first man he trained was "a master of the business," but he was taken sick in the campaign of 1776 at New York, and Bushnell was obliged to find another volunteer. Under the direction of Sergeant Ezra Lee, the "Turtle" made an attack upon the 64-gun ship Eagle in New York harbor. The British vessel was at anchor and Lee successfully navigated the submarine under her. In attempting to fix the wooden screw into her bottom, however, he struck a bar of iron. He sought another place in the ship's hull, but, "not being well skilled in the management of the vessel," he lost the Eagle. After seeking her for some time under water, Lee was compelled to come to the surface, where he made good his escape, without the magazine, however, which exploded off Governor's Island to the consternation of the enemy.

Two subsequent attacks were made against British ships with the submarine. In one of these the operator succeeded in placing the "Turtle" under the hostile man-of-war, but the tide ran so strong that the little vessel was swept away, and nothing further could be done before the enemy came up the river and unsuspectingly pursued and sunk a vessel which had their dread enemy on board. Bushnell tells us that he later recovered his submarine, "but found it impossible to prosecute the design further."

In the following winter Bushnell exhibited a new invention "for annoying ships" to the Governor and Council of Connecticut. It was a floating torpedo in the shape of a keg, designed to explode by contact. His first attempt was made in the Delaware River, and the alarm of the British soldiery on that memorable Christmas night was the inspiration of the song of "The Battle of the Kegs."

David Bushnell served throughout the Revolutionary War as captain in the corps of sappers and miners. At his death, an unfinished model, evidently that of a torpedo, was found among his effects, which showed that, notwithstanding his disappointments, his mind still clung to his life's work.

II. THE COTTON GIN

(ELI WHITNEY, Class of 1792)

By

JOSEPH W. ROE

Eli Whitney was born on a farm in Westboro, Massachusetts, in 1765, and graduated at Yale in 1792. His attention was turned to the cotton gin in the fall of 1792, through a conversation with a number of planters who were visiting the widow of General Nathaniel Greene, near Savannah.

The cultivation of long staple cotton had begun seven years before, but its production was confined to the Sea Islands, and was, therefore, sharply limited. The short staple or green cotton could be grown throughout the South but was commercially valueless unless an efficient means were developed for separating the staple from the seed. With the hand methods then known, the cleaning of a single pound constituted a day's work.

Whitney secured some raw cotton, attacked the problem, and within a few weeks had developed the cotton gin which has remained almost unchanged in its essential elements to this day. The effect of the invention was immediate and far-reaching. In 1784, eight bales of cotton had been seized by the customs authorities at Liverpool on the ground that they could not have been produced in the United States. From less than $\frac{1}{250}$ of the world's supply, the American crop rose in one generation to over $\frac{7}{8}$. It made the prosperity of the South, and indirectly but very materially affected New England and, in fact, the whole country. But the very value of the invention made it almost impossible for Whitney to defend his patent against infringement.   He became involved in numberless suits, and only after years of litigation established his claims and succeeded in obtaining from various sources amounts which, all told, about equaled his expenses.

Recognizing that he would never receive an adequate return from the cotton gin, he turned to the manufacture of an unpatented article, by new methods, in a shop which was open to all. In 1798 he obtained a contract for 10,000 muskets for the United States Government, established the Whitney Arms Company in New Haven, and developed there the modern interchangeable system of manufacture.   While he was not the first to propose this system, he was the first to make it a commercial success, and to demonstrate that articles could be produced not only interchangeably but at prices even cheaper than by the old hand methods.   In doing so he developed the commercial use of jigs, fixtures, and limit gauges, and made the beginnings of a number of important modern machine tools.

Simeon North, a gunsmith of Middletown, Connecticut, shared with Whitney to some degree in this work, and with them modern interchangeable manufacture had its inception.   Of the two, Whitney was by far the more influential.   From their shops interchangeable methods spread to other gun makers, to the clock makers, and later, as they were developed, to other industries, such as the manufacture of sewing machines, typewriters, and bicycles.   The skill of the New England mechanics in this type of manufacture has had much to do with the manufacturing supremacy of the United States.

Whitney's invention of the cotton gin is well known and its tremendous economic effect is universally recognized.   Few, however, realize that he affected modern industry almost as profoundly in a second and entirely different field.   Eli Whitney was a wise, far-seeing business man, a great mechanic, and an inventor who contributed immeasurably to the agricultural and manufacturing wealth of the nineteenth century.   Robert Fulton placed him with Arkwright and Watt as one of the three of his contemporaries who had done most for mankind.

III. THE TELEGRAPH

(SAMUEL FINLEY BREESE MORSE, Class of 1810)

By

EDWARD L. MORSE

The story of the invention of the Telegraph by Samuel F. B. Morse is too well-known to need detailed description, but certain essentials of the invention cannot be too often nor too strongly emphasized, and certain other facts will be of particular interest to all Yale men.

It was while Morse was a student at Yale, from which he graduated in 1810, that the seed was sown which eventually grew and bore fruit in one of the epoch-making inventions of the world. Under Professors Day and Silliman he was introduced to that mysterious fluid which, in later years, he was to be the first to tame to the use of man. On March 8th, 1809, he writes to his parents:—"Mr. Day's lectures are very interesting. They are upon Electricity. The whole class taking hold of hands, formed the circuit of communication, and we all received the shock apparently at the same moment." This was the germ which, lying dormant for over twenty years, finally took root and burst into glorious flower, and to Yale is granted the proud privilege of having planted that seed.

The actual invention, as everyone knows, occurred on board the packet-ship Sully in October, 1832. The essentials were very simple but were entirely different from any other form of telegraph devised by others. It was their very simplicity which compelled the admiration of scientists and practical men of affairs alike, and gradually forced into desuetude all other systems, until to-day the Morse Telegraph still maintains its position as the universal telegraph.

For more than ten years Morse worked, at first alone and then with the legitimate assistance of others, not only to perfect his system but to compel a skeptical generation to acknowledge its practicability, and on May 24th, 1844, the historic message, "What hath God wrought!" was flashed over the completed line from Washington to Baltimore.

A brief summary of Morse's inventions and discoveries follows. In October, 1832, he conceived the idea of his telegraph. In 1835-6 and 7 he produced actual results by mechanism constructed solely by himself. He devised in 1832 the dot-and-dash system which, in 1835 or 1836, he perfected, thereby producing the "Morse Alphabet." In 1836 he discovered the principle of the relay. In 1838 he received a French patent for a system of railway telegraph which also embodies the principle of the police and fire-alarm telegraph. At the same time he suggested a practical form of military telegraph. In 1842 he laid the first sub-aqueous cable. In 1842 he discovered, with Dr. Fisher, the principle of duplex telegraphy, and in the same year he was the first to experiment with wireless telegraphy.

It was the Morse system which first demonstrated the actual practicability of controlling to the uses of man what was, up to that time, a little understood plaything of the laboratory, and this in turn impelled other men of genius to broaden its field of usefulness, so that we may truthfully say that it was Morse who ushered in the present Age of Electricity.

SAMUEL FINLEY BREESE MORSE
Class of 1810

IV. THE STONE BREAKER

(ELI WHITNEY BLAKE, Class of 1816)

By

HENRY T. BLAKE

"The Blake Stone Breaker" invented by Eli Whitney Blake (Yale 1816) is so well known throughout the world, as a leading, if not a principal, agency in creating and developing during the last fifty years the "Era of Good Roads" and the no less important "Age of Concrete," as well as the remarkable growth of mining and other enterprises which embrace the use of broken stone, that a discourse on its value would be superfluous. Hence I have been asked to present not an essay on the importance of the invention but merely a brief account of the circumstances of its origin and the manner in which it developed in the mind of the inventor. These points are always interesting features in the history of any new and valuable invention, and help to determine what measure of honor and gratitude is due to its author.

Fortunately in this case we have the inventor's own story of his achievement in the sworn statement submitted by him to the Commissioner of Patents, in 1872, on his application for an extension of his patent; the law then requiring that in such a petition the applicant should show among other things the labor which the invention had cost him and also its value to the public.

"My Stone Breaker," he says, "is a machine so simple and one the whole theory of which is so readily comprehended at a glance that many have thought it could have cost little or no trouble to invent it, and that it may have been the result of a single happy thought coming into my mind unsought. On the contrary the invention was the fruit of years of earnest and persistent thought, study and research, specially devoted to that object." He then states that his attention was first called to the public need of such a machine through his appointment in 1851 by the City of New Haven on a Committee to construct two miles of macadam road on one of the City avenues—"At which time," he says, "I believe there were not a dozen miles of macadam road in all the New England States." He declares that he devoted himself at once to a careful study of all the books that he could obtain on the subject, and "found that no way had been devised to break stone into fragments except by hand hammers requiring two days' labor to produce only a cubic yard of road-metal and that in coarser fragments than was desirable for a good road bed." He adds, "the importance of a machine to do the work became immediately obvious and from that time for a period of seven years scarcely a day or an hour passed in which my mind was not mainly occupied with the subject."

On careful reflection he saw that the problem before him was to contrive an apparatus which should act at the same time on a considerable number of stones of different sizes and shapes, and from which all such fragments as had been at any time reduced to the desired size should be rapidly and automatically removed. "To this problem," he says, "I devoted my thoughts revolving it in my mind almost constantly day and night. More than three years had passed in this way before I had formed a full and distinct idea of the simple device whereby this mode of operation is effected in my patented machine, to wit: a pair of upright converging jaws far enough apart at the top to receive the stones to be broken; near enough together at the bottom to prevent the falling out of such fragments as require farther reduction and one of the jaws to have a short vibrating movement towards and from the other."

The principle of operation having thus been decided on, it still remained to organize a machine embodying the principle and adapted for practical use. Such a machine must be sufficiently small and compact for transportation and use in the roughest localities and capable of quick, easy, and cheap repair in case of breakage. The vibrating jaw also which was to exert a pressure of 27,000 lbs. per square inch on its usual trap rock contents must be actuated by some device combining the greatest amount of power with the least amount of friction; and the entire apparatus must be enclosed in some frame work capable of enduring indefinitely the enormous strain to which such work must subject it. The study and computations involved in this part of the invention occupied four years more of constant thought and labor before they resulted in a combination of lever, toggle-joint, and fly wheel contained in a massive, solid iron frame; a combination which for its simplicity and effectiveness has often been referred to by experts as a notable mechanical achievement.

After the general design of the machine had thus been arrived at, its construction came next in order. The form and strength of every part was worked out in detail on paper before a step in construction was taken, and so carefully was this done that the first machine set up proved to be as perfect in all working qualities as the one that has been last produced after fifty years of experience. It only remains to add that the last Stone Breaker which has been made up to the present day by any maker throughout the world differs in no essential particular from that experimental machine which was constructed by the inventor in 1858.

YALE IN ENGINEERING AND MANUFACTURING

By

JAMES F. McCLELLAND

Yale College in 1716 was wholly academic in spirit. Its degrees recognized solely the arts. The trend of its teaching was clearly classical. The first impulse of its graduates was towards the ministry. Yale University in 1916 recognizes equally the arts and the sciences. Between its two great undergraduate departments—Academic and Scientific—there is no marked disparity in numbers. It awards numerous higher degrees in science and engineering. The curriculum even of the Academic Department requires the sciences at least to supplement the arts. In an age increasingly scientific and industrial, the tendency of Yale graduates is more and more towards such occupations as engineering and manufacturing.

The intention of the present discussion is chiefly to recognize in the modern development of Yale University the scope and significance in her scheme of liberal education of the engineering and allied courses, to note her laboratories and other facilities for technical instruction, and to suggest the practical effects of this training on the choice of occupation of Yale graduates. It is not the intention to review in detail the history of a progress so recent and so rapid that its most important chapters are being written in the lives of living men. The imprint of Yale names on some of the leading engineering and manufacturing organizations of to-day is a matter of common knowledge, while the list of those whose guidance, if less outwardly conspicuous, is hardly less important, in the management of similar industries and interests would be impressive.

Probably no better evidence, however, of the general contribution of Yale to such occupations as engineering and manufacturing can be found than in the statistics given in the latest [1914] issue of the *Directory of Living Graduates*. In the summaries showing the distribution by occupation of living Yale graduates the net totals for manufacturing (2,072) and for engineering (1,991) are exceeded only by that for law (3,901). Education, which only two years previous, in 1912, outranked both, is now outnumbered by both. After education, in the 1914 summaries, there follow immediately finance (1,882) and mercantile business (1,461), while among the smaller groups transportation (236) is almost equal in numbers to art (244). To recall that a century ago (taking the figures for the classes of 1805-1815), the three so-called learned professions—law, ministry, and medicine—each outnumbered individually the total included under so broad a classification as "business," is to emphasize the contrast between past and present. Even the fact that, out of somewhat more than 18,000 living Yale graduates in 1914 over 4,000 were listed as engaged in engineering or manufacturing, and that over 3,300 others were in finance or mercantile business, fails to show adequately the trend of the times. So rapid are the present percentages of increase that the forthcoming *Directory* of 1916 will doubtless prove these illustrations underdrawn.

It is natural to turn from "Yale in Engineering and Manufacturing" to "Engineering in Yale." The founding in 1846 of a "School of Applied Chemistry" as a part of what has now become the Sheffield Scientific School was closely followed by the establishment in 1852 of a "School of Engineering." From the outset engineering was a leading factor in the incipient Scientific School—then known as the "Department of Philosophy and the Arts." Present methods and facilities for training in its various branches are the result of steady progress along the broad lines adopted early. In 1860, the undergraduate course in engineering was of two years' duration; the successful completion of an additional year of graduate work led to the degree of Civil Engineer. Since 1866 the undergraduate course has occupied three years.   Separate departments and courses of instruction in mechanical, electrical, mining, and metallurgical engineering were established as the school grew.   This expansion kept pace with the rapid growth of engineering knowledge and the consequent demand on scientific and technical schools to enlarge the scope of the training offered.   These conditions also resulted in increasing the period of graduate study required for the higher engineering degrees to two years.   For a long time past, the student desiring to obtain from Yale the degree of Engineer has devoted a total of five years of study to that task, although, in some departments, two or more years of creditable field work are accepted in lieu of one of the resident graduate years.   Throughout the development of the engineering side of the Sheffield Scientific School, there has been a firm insistence that the student shall acquire a full understanding of the sciences fundamental to engineering work, together with an adequate knowledge of such humanities as English and modern languages.   In general the application of fundamental subjects to technical problems is deferred until the graduate years.   The wisdom of laying a firm foundation before building up a superstructure of technical knowledge is shown by the marked success of many men who have taken only the undergraduate degree.

Recent progress has been along lines of correlating more closely the work of the four engineering departments and of strengthening the courses of instruction in fundamental subjects.   The erection of three engineering laboratories since 1905, all made possible through the generosity of alumni, also marks a new era of advance.   The Hammond Laboratory is equipped for instruction in mining and metallurgy and allied subjects; the Mason Laboratory provides facilities for experimental work in steam and gas engineering, testing materials, and other branches of mechanical engineering; the Electrical Laboratory is furnished with equipment for both elementary and advanced instruction in the various details of electrical engineering.   The Civil Engineering department in 1913 secured a tract of more than one thousand acres of land at East Lyme, Connecticut, to serve as a field laboratory for work in surveying and hydraulics. These laboratories stand for increased opportunities in experimental work so valuable to the undergraduate and absolutely necessary to the student seeking the more specialized knowledge and experience that go with the engineering degrees. They have also made it possible to undertake investigations of processes and machines for manufacturers and others who have neither adequate laboratory facilities nor trained research men of their own. At present ten graduate students are being maintained at these laboratories by various manufacturing companies to investigate special problems and to receive training as research workers. The recently inaugurated courses in Business Administration, covering a year of graduate study, likewise broaden the scope of the training offered to men who desire eventually to attain executive positions in engineering or allied work.

Practical evidence of the wide interest taken by graduates of the University in engineering development at Yale is found in the Yale Engineering Association. This organization was founded in 1914 under the direction of some of Yale's most prominent graduates connected with engineering and manufacturing interests. The objects of the association, whose membership is open to all holders of Yale degrees, as stated in its constitution are as follows:

To advance the interests of engineering education at Yale, to promote the better acquaintance and fellowship of Yale engineers; to establish closer relations and coöperation between the engineering departments of the Sheffield Scientific School and Yale graduates engaged in active engineering practice; to bring together the older graduates, already established, and the younger men entering upon their professional work, and to take such other action as from time to time may seem advisable to promote the welfare of engineering interests at Yale and of Yale engineers.

This association with a membership of between seven and eight hundred is the largest group of Yale alumni organized for the specific purpose of aiding one of the departments of the University.

The interest of Yale in engineering is not, however, departmental. In 1914, 281 of its living academical graduates had entered it as their occupation, together with graduates of all other departments of the University save those of Music and Fine Arts. Even more noteworthy is the case of manufacturing, where the number from Yale College (982) almost equals that from the Sheffield Scientific School (1,045). Such proofs are conclusive that engineering and manufacturing, together with other occupations of the modern business world, have become an integral part of the University idea as exemplified both within the University itself and in the careers of Yale alumni in the world outside.

YALE IN FORESTRY

By

GIFFORD PINCHOT

During the period of growing but sporadic interest in forestry which preceded the establishment of a National Forest policy, Yale played an honorable and an important part. Professor William H. Brewer prepared for the census the first forest map of the United States, and did much, both at that time, and when he afterwards became a member of the Forest Commission of the National Academy of Sciences, to awaken the people of the United States to the value of forests as sources of wood, water, and public health. His experiments upon the durability of woods extended over a period of forty years. Edward H. Bowers, now lecturer in forest law at the Yale Forest School, took, as assistant commissioner of the General Land Office, and as one of the directing members of the American Forestry Association, an important part in securing the passage of the Act of 1891, which authorized the creation of the National Forests, and of the act of 1897, which provided the authority for practical forest management upon them. In addition to Professor Brewer, Doctor Arnold Hague, '63 S., of the U. S. Geological Survey, was a member of the National Forest Commission, and Gifford Pinchot, '89, was a member and its Secretary. Doctor Hague laid down the boundaries of the first National Forest, and for many years has been influential in the movement for forest preservation in the West.

When in July, 1898, the writer was appointed as head of the Division of Forestry (now the United States Forest Service) in the Department of Agriculture at Washington, it became evident at once that success was impossible in the absence of a supply of professionally trained foresters. To meet this need the Yale Forest School was established in 1900. The first Director of the Yale Forest School was Professor Henry S. Graves, now at the head of the United States Forest Service. When Professor Graves left the old Division of Forestry, of which he was Assistant Chief, to undertake the work of establishing the School at Yale, the knowledge necessary for professional teaching in forestry had not been assembled in text books. What had been acquired was widely scattered, and indeed much of it did not yet exist at all. His task at first was not merely to organize and direct the School, but also to assemble the material of instruction, prepare it for presentation, and present it to the students. Most important of all, and most difficult, it was imperative to establish with these incomplete tools a high standard of professional achievement, instruction, and esprit de corps among the students of the school, and to maintain it in a community when forestry as a profession was as yet substantially unknown. His successful accomplishment of all these tasks constitutes one of the greatest and most difficult services that has yet been rendered to the cause of forestry in the United States.

When Professor Graves left the Yale Forest School to become the head of the United States Forest Service, he was succeeded as Director by Professor James W. Toumey, a former member of the Forest Service, and the associate of Professor Graves for many years at Yale. To him is due the further progress and present admirable efficiency of the Yale Forest School.

One other forest school had been established before the School at Yale and one established during the same year was later discontinued, but has recently resumed its work. The Yale Forest School is the oldest school in the United States with an unbroken history, and it has furnished for the work of forestry a larger, and it is well within the truth to say, a far more influential body of graduates than any other forest school in the country. During its existence of fifteen years, the Yale Forest School has graduated 344 men with the degree of Master of Forestry, and in addition 120 men, who did not complete work enough to entitle them to a degree, have been prepared in part for the practice of forestry. Its students have come from all portions of the United States and from foreign countries. In a single class, graduates from 21 American colleges have been included. England, Germany, Norway, Sweden, Canada, South Africa, the Sandwich Islands, the Philippine Islands, China, and Japan have sent forest students to Yale. The services of the School, its influence, and its position are not merely national but international.

There are at present in the United States Forest Service 153 men trained at Yale. Of the twenty states which have organized departments of forestry under technically trained men, twelve are directed by former students of the Yale Forest School, while ten additional graduates hold less important positions in state forestry.

The departments or schools of forestry in Cornell University, Harvard University, the University of Maine, the University of Minnesota, Syracuse University, Colorado Agricultural College, Michigan Agricultural College, the State College of Pennsylvania, the University of Washington, and the State College of Washington are directed by graduates of the Yale Forest School. Other institutions which have Yale men upon the teaching staff in forestry are the University of California, the University of Missouri, the Massachusetts Agricultural College, and the New Hampshire College. Twenty-eight graduates of the Yale Forest School are directors, professors, or assistant professors on the faculties of departments of forestry or schools of forestry in the fourteen educational institutions in this country which offer technical training in forestry leading to a professional degree. The exertion of so commanding an influence upon the profession for which it prepares is probably unequaled in its sphere by any other professional school of any kind in the United States.

Graduates of the Yale Forest School are at the head of the forest service in the Philippine Islands, the Sandwich Islands, the province of Quebec, and the province of British Columbia, and are in charge of forest schools in New Brunswick, Quebec, and South Africa. Nine graduates of the School are engaged in professional work in the Philippine Islands, two in China, two in South Africa, and eleven in Canada. Members of its faculty are on the governing boards of all the forestry associations of national character in America, and on the editorial boards of the three forest journals which are not local in character.

It is a remarkable fact, and thoroughly indicative of the position and influence of the Yale Forest School in the establishment and maintenance of forestry in the United States, that nearly two-thirds of the professional text books on forestry published in this country in the last fifteen years were written by members of the faculty of this school or by its graduates.

ART AT YALE

By

JOHN F. WEIR

In 1863 Augustus Russell Street, a graduate of Yale of the Class of 1812, signified to the college authorities his desire to erect upon the college square a large and appropriate building adapted to the purposes of a School of the Fine Arts. Three objects were prominent in the plan of this liberal-minded benefactor: first, to provide a school of technical training for those proposing to follow art professionally as painters, sculptors, or architects; second, to provide courses of lectures in the history and criticism of art in all its branches, adapted to the need of professional students and undergraduates; and third, to provide for the community at large, including the university and the city, such familiarity with works of art as may be derived from loan-exhibitions and permanent collections.

Mr. Street was the first to give practical form to the conception that the study of the Fine Arts properly comes within the scope of a university. His aim was not simply to establish a museum of art, which alone had found place in this connection in a few foreign universities, but to provide technical schools of practice with professional aims.

When the founder of this department declined to have his name connected with the title of the institution, modestly suggesting that it be named the "Yale School of the Fine Arts," it was partly with the idea that future gifts contributing to its development would be free of the hindrance that sometimes attaches to institutions bearing a founder's name. The foundation-stone was laid in 1864, and the building was completed in 1867 at a cost of $220,000; while Mrs. Street's gifts, after the death of her husband (who did not live to see the building completed), amounted to above $85,000 more, principally for the endowment of chairs of instruction.

Yale had already, in 1831, manifested an interest in art by the purchase of the Trumbull collection of historical paintings and portraits of the period of the American Revolution. This was a notable act under the circumstances, quite in advance of ideas then prevalent in similar institutions. The organization of the School of Fine Arts was begun through the endowment of a professorship of painting and design, to which was attached the directorship of the School in accordance with the terms of the original project. This office was filled in 1869, and at the same time a professor of the history and criticism of art was appointed, who entered upon his duties two years later. With the appointment of a Director the School opened at the beginning of the Fall Term of 1869 with an attendance of four students in the technical courses then provided. In 1871 a foundation was received for a professorship of drawing; and through arrangements made with other departments of the University for giving instruction in art to undergraduates, the annual attendance of students of all classes eventually rose, in succeeding years, to upwards of four hundred; while the teaching-force was increased to seven instructors. Classes were formed in drawing, painting, sculpture, and architecture; in composition, perspective, and anatomy; and in the history and criticism of art. The total number of students of various classes who have studied in the School from 1869 to the present time, is above eight thousand. Annual loan-exhibitions were held in connection with the general objects of the School, while courses of public lectures were provided, principally by persons distinguished in the profession as painters, sculptors, or architects; also by the leading critics of the day, and other writers on art.

Among the endowments of the School that should be mentioned is that of the Winchester Fellowship, yielding an annual income of $1,000, for supplementing the courses in painting, sculpture or architecture, by sending the successful competitor abroad for two years to be passed in the art schools of Paris. Finding, ultimately, that the technical instruction given in the Yale Art School appeared to equal that received abroad, the competition for this fellowship was held annually, sending the student abroad for one year; on his return he is required to pass an additional year in an advanced course here, ending in the degree of Bachelor of Fine Arts conferred by the University. An endowment was also received for a traveling-scholarship, known as the English Scholarship, open to competition; which sends the successful student abroad for the summer vacation, under the supervision of the faculty as to the course to be pursued. An endowment, recently increased, was also received for a course of public lectures on art, known as the Trowbridge Course.

Among the acquisitions that comprise what may now properly be termed the Yale Art Museum, is the Jarves Collection of Italian paintings, dating from the 11th to the 17th century, numbering one hundred and twenty examples; which was purchased in 1871. Also the Alden Wood-Carvings of the 17th century, comprising three confessionals and some eight hundred square feet of carved oak wainscoting from the Chapel of a suppressed convent in Ghent, purchased in 1897. Also a Collection of Casts from Greek, Roman, and Renaissance sculptures filling one of the large galleries. The purchase of these collections, instead of relying upon gifts, is what has given to the Yale Art Museum a unique distinction.

Among the important gifts to the School was one in 1911, of $60,000, from a friend of the institution, which was partly applied as an endowment in the department of architecture, and more largely in the erection of an annex to the original Street building as a memorial to the late Richard S. Fellowes, a graduate of Yale of the Class of 1832. This fire-proof structure added three new exhibition-galleries and six class-rooms to the School, making its structural plant consist of five exhibition-galleries and seventeen other apartments, including a library, lecture-room, drawing, painting, modeling, and architectural class rooms, and studios for instructors. A like sum, namely $60,000 (subject to a life-annuity), was bequeathed to the School by Professor Hoppin, late professor in the history of art, for the endowment, when available, of a professorship in architecture. It may be proper to state that pecuniary gifts to this Department of the University for buildings, endowments, and other objects, have amounted to above $600,000.

Something should be said of the system of instruction emphasized as appropriate to a School of the Fine Arts that takes its place beside other professional schools in the University. What is known as the academic system is the one most adequate for securing thoroughness of training in these arts, by its disciplining the faculties most widely active in the production of art; adding to the technical practice a knowledge of the historic standards; revealing the types as fundamentally fixed in art, as science reveals them fixed in nature; originality consisting in variations based on the type through new forms of selection and arrangement, and new methods of technique. A knowledge of the historic standards broadens and enriches the mind of the artist by storing it with materials applicable in the professional practice; and in common with other interests of the intellectual life this knowledge should receive its proper emphasis in a School of the Fine Arts included within the scheme of a great University.

YALE IN ARCHITECTURE

By

GROSVENOR ATTERBURY

To an Art which is called upon to express almost every phase of a nation's activities and aspirations, the contribution of a university may be correspondingly varied. It may be confined to the stimulation in the student body of that natural sense of beauty which exists to some extent in every normal human—an influence which can be the result both of class-room teaching and the architectural atmosphere of the university. Or, working more directly, its contribution may consist in the technical work of its laboratories in those sciences which are so intimately bound up with the Art of Architecture. But, most directly of all, its contribution may be made through the work of those graduates who, in the practice of the Art, formulate and solve in architectural language—in wood, brick, stone, and steel,—the problems of the Body Social of their day;—the men who make its sense of beauty articulate, crystallize its esthetic tendencies, and stimulate its finest aspirations.

In appraising Yale's service to the cause of American architecture it must be remembered that she has but recently passed out of that period of education when the recipe for the curriculum might well have read, as suggested by one of her ablest teachers:—"One cup of Latin, one cup of Greek, one cup of Mathematics, one tablespoonful of Philosophy, and a pinch of History." It must be remembered also that during the two hundred years reviewed in our Pageant she has represented more fully than any other college the broad average of Americanism, drawing her students from all corners of the continent as none of her sister universities have done. Now both the Puritanic curriculum and Yale's democracy spell Philistinism. As a people we are but just laying the foundations of that sense and love of Beauty that will some day glorify the structure of our final nationality,—as the sense and love of Liberty inspired its conception. Let us not deceive ourselves into thinking that we are as yet a cultured people. The American wilderness was not conquered by Japanese prints. Our fathers of six generations ago were not art collectors but Indian fighters. So, in our Pageant, when you see the "Arts and Sciences" entering the stage of the arena in glorious state immediately after the founding of New Haven and Yale, you must remember that in all allegories like this there is considerable license permitted—even under the "Blue Laws" of Connecticut.

As a matter of fact, the emigrating Arts and Sciences fell on evil days. Rightly enough the appeal for morality preceded that for beauty, though they are but different forms of the same principle. So the concept of visual beauty was left to be developed by the few who called themselves artists. In the case of our architecture, this work was until recently relegated to the man whose sign read "Builder and Architect—Jobbing Promptly Attended To." When you think of it, this is not so surprising in the case of a young people set down on a vast undeveloped continent where naturally enough their first business has been the garnering of certain very material elements in the pursuit of happiness. So likewise it is not to be wondered at that throughout the country as a whole (most universities included) there is still to-day such a woeful lack of a decent respect for the opinions of architects. For truly it is only within a generation that there has been any considerable number of architects who deserved respect. As a trained profession we are still in our first generation: with a wilderness full of savage tastes to conquer:—still struggling to free ourselves from the mantle of the jerry-builder and from a rather widespread belief that you have only to scratch an architect to find a plumber.

What then has been Yale's part in all this? In this generation she can claim a score of men, some of whose names should rank high when the final balance is struck in the years to come; but in the past her record, we must confess, is a barren one. For this doubtless Yale has her Puritan ancestry to thank. In her younger days, art was "Anathema:" her founders thought they disliked it; abjured it as they did kissing on the Sabbath. How long their Blue Laws kept their original color intact I do not know. One has suspicions. But from the beginning the sense of beauty, at any rate, began to push its way out from beneath the mask. Even in the days of Rector Pierson the impulse could not be entirely suppressed. I dare say it showed itself on the very porch in Killingworth under which he read "Ames' *Cases of Conscience*" to the assembled collegians—quite three in number. Thus, bits of charming cornice, little runs of dentils and decorative window heads made their silent appeal—plain evidences of the spirit of beauty which could not be suppressed,—shy, hesitant, refined, utterly charming, yet persistent—like wild flowers pushing up between city flagstones. And it is just these little mannerisms of the old Colonial work which furnish even to-day the most natural inspiration for an American architecture.

So Yale officially hardened her conscience against Art, while the homes of the men who taught and studied there, despite their prim simplicity, were instinct with the craving for it. Graceful, even playful, lines in chair backs, mirror heads, and leaded fan lights were the tiny springs, the native source of our Colonial architecture,—just as the spires of the two churches on the Green point to its high-water mark.

Were Yale's contribution to American architecture to be based on distinguished performances or individual performers we should make a sorry showing. But the character of a nation's architecture is not determined alone by its monumental buildings, outstanding for their exceptional merits, but rather by the average of its total product. And if Yale's esthetic standing has suffered from her pronounced democracy, the same cause makes her opportunities to serve the cause of art greater perhaps than those of some of her sister universities whose student bodies represent a

whom he naturally admired; moreover, he was a composer of verse as well as of music and his influence must have been altogether benign. Some of his compositions had a wide use after the middle of the century. In a sketch of his college years he writes thus of the Beethoven Society:

A society which oftener went by the simple name of College Choir and was composed of both voices and instruments. The organ, at that period, was not. The sacred violin, in those years, took the place of the 'kist o' whistles!' We had, besides, flutes, tenor violins, double-bass and 'cello; we had a most sonorous ophicleide (which was blown out the Chapel windows for rehearsals, to the conviction of delinquent members), we had a big drum, but that was a luxury—for exceptional effects; we had numerous guitars and Brazilian mandolins (in reserve); and had a jew's-harp presented itself for examination, and had it passed on a solemn church tune of good and regular standing, such was the breadth and catholicity of our musical views, that I doubt not the harp of ancient, ecclesiastical allusion, would have been one of us.

The serious study of music, in the sense which modern musicians accept, began with Gustave J. Stoeckel. Mr. Stoeckel was born in Bavaria in 1819, was principal of the High School in Landstuhl in 1848, when he incurred governmental displeasure on account of his liberal ideas, and came to the United States. In 1854, Mr. Joseph Battell established a fund for the support of a teacher of the Science of Music, and Mr. Stoeckel was appointed to fulfill the requirements of this endowment; first, Instructor in Vocal Music, and later Chapel-Master and Organist. Upon his assumption of these offices, music for mixed voices was abandoned and only such as was proper for male voices used in the choir and glee club, both of which Mr. Stoeckel directed.

Mr. Stoeckel was thoroughly in sympathy with the rapid advance in musical culture which marked his time and manfully bore his part therein. Perhaps his most important undertaking was the Beethoven Festival of 1870, to commemorate the 100th anniversary of the composer's birth. The Festival took place December 5th, 6th, and 7th. There were three evening and two afternoon concerts, given by an orchestra of sixty-five men, a chorus of one hundred and seventy-five choir singers from New Haven and Hartford, and soloists. All the works performed were by Beethoven. Yale conferred the degree of Doctor of Music upon Mr. Stoeckel in 1864, and his musical activities continued for full thirty years thereafter, when he retired. As organist, teacher, conductor, composer, and as first Professor of Music at Yale, his name and work should be held in honor.

Yale musicians are indebted to Mr. Joel Sumner Smith (Yale 1853) of the Library, for his constant, intelligent interest in musical activities, for his unselfish labors and numerous contributions to the University Library of works in many languages, chiefly Slavonic, on folk lore or folk music. The catalogue of the Lowell Mason Library of about nine thousand titles, given to the College by Lowell Mason's widow, is in his handwriting.

Following the retirement of Dr. Stoeckel, the present writer was appointed Battell Professor of the Theory of Music; Samuel Simons Sanford, Professor of Applied Music; and Harry Benjamin Jepson, College, later University, Organist. For many reasons it was deemed wise at this time to include Practical Music as an elective in the college courses and credit has been given for such studies ever since then. Professor Sanford's genial personality and eminent musicianship were a constant source of enjoyment and profit to those students who were in contact with him. His daughter, Mrs. George M. Landers, has given since 1912 the Samuel Simons Sanford Fellowship, for two years' study of music abroad.

In 1894 the New Haven Symphony Orchestra began its career under University auspices. Since then it has given a series of orchestral concerts every year, thereby bringing to the University and to the city a mass of the best music which otherwise would largely have remained unheard. Although this service is valuable, it is not the main reason for such concerts or for the orchestra.

We undertake to teach the composition of music to our students who are able to profit by such teaching. The coördination of Theory and Practice, a familiar need in most studies, is indispensable in the higher branches of music. It is possible to give students very exact theoretical training, to teach them how to write correctly for orchestra. But given a student of talent and promise, who has composed something worth hearing, it is likely to hinder or to end his progress as a composer if he is forced to go forth seeking an orchestra with charity or leisure enough to play it for him. Except for philanthropic reasons it is not likely to be played. But he must hear it before he can know what he has written. Only the physical impact upon his own ears of the tones and tone-combinations conceived in his mind, can coördinate what he has learned with what he has imagined. Furthermore, the knowledge that his work will actually be played is a tremendous incentive to compose. Every year we are able to send forth students equipped with this experience; not many, not often more than one or two, but they have learned to tread the path which leads to the higher regions of music. It is as a laboratory for such that I believe the orchestra fulfills its highest function.

Three people are indispensable to all music-making; first, the composer, or producer; second, the performer, or reproducer; and third, the listener to whom the efforts of the other two are addressed. We provide for all three classes, for composers by our theoretical training, for performers by teaching students how to play or sing, and for the largest class, the listeners, by lectures on the history and the nature of music, and, better still, by concerts.

A new building has been given for the School of Music, by Mrs. Albert Arnold Sprague, in memory of her husband (Yale 1859), which is to bring nearly all our activities under one roof. So far we have had no single room which was made for our purposes. We hope that this much-needed home will give a new impetus to the study and practice of music at Yale, and that it may help to make the name of the University noteworthy in the development of musical knowledge and culture.

YALE AND THE DRAMA

By

JAMES S. METCALFE

In a fable of Turgueniev it is narrated that the good God once gave a party in his Temple of Azure to all the virtues, both great and small. He observed that among those present there were two ladies who did not speak. Taking one of them by the hand He presented her to the other. "Gratitude, this is Benevolence," He said. Since the beginning of the world the two had never met. This fable is recalled in attempting to write of Yale and the Drama.

American colleges and universities have made few contributions to dramatic literature. They have been mostly under the influence and control of religious denominations that have regarded the theatre as a frivolous and worldly institution to be condemned, or at least ignored. Preparation for the pulpit they have always considered a principal employment for their energies. To take cognizance of the great possibilities of the stage as a channel of popular and moral education has never occurred to a single one of our great educational institutions.

Yale, being in its foundations essentially religious, has entirely neglected, until very recently, the existence of the modern drama. In the Greek courses it has had to recognize the drama of Greece, not because it was drama, but because it was literature. For the same reason attention has been directed to the dramatic classics of England and France. In Yale's teaching, however, these products of the great minds of the past have been included only as examples of literary culture, never as suggesting the possibilities of the appeal of the spoken play. As an institution, Yale has not even followed the example of some of the foreign universities in encouraging the actual performance of the classic plays its instructors used on account of the literary value of their text. In this neglect of the living drama and the theatre Yale has not been in any way an exception, but has abided by the practice in all other American educational institutions with a religious bias.

It is not strange, then, that so far as the theatre is concerned, Yale is a negative influence. It is only lately that any American university has included in its curriculum any teaching that could have influence in shaping the literature which, night after night, the year around, is conveying over the footlights to the whole American people a true or false education, a refined or vulgar culture. Harvard, with only slight exertion, has shown that a university can do much when it turns any part of its energies in this direction. Yale, so far, has made little effort in this field of education, so that to speak or write of Yale and the Drama is to treat of a connection that does not exist. Nowhere in the history of the American theatre, its control, its acting, or its literature does the name of Yale appear. In the revival of the art of pageantry, which is closely allied to the art of the theatre, Yale has made its influence felt in a way that bodes well for the place of the university in the future history of the American drama.

The wisest and most potent effort that Yale has made in the matter of dramatic education is the recently-established influence in directing undergraduate activity towards what is of value in a dramatic way instead of letting it follow its natural bent towards the entirely frivolous. It is quite natural that the undergraduate should want to play-act. Every observer of human nature, even of animal nature, recognizes the universal presence of this desire. Yale men of earlier generations know how it found its vent in the saturnalia of the Thanksgiving Jubilee and in the crude efforts of the societies. Now it is finding a legitimate, and in many ways profitable sphere of action, in the intelligently directed accomplishments of the Yale University Dramatic Association. In no other American university or college is this activity so wisely guided. When to it is joined a wider interest in the literary study of the modern drama and in the possibilities of the theatre of to-day regarded as an educational and artistic institution, results are bound to come which will give material to the future writer and, if he is a Yale man, pride in discoursing on Yale and the Drama. Yale needs the drama and the theatre for its broadening influence, and the American theatre needs Yale not only in its drama, but in every branch of its many activities.

YA-LI
THE COLLEGE OF YALE IN CHINA

By

FREDERICK WELLS WILLIAMS

The Scholar Gipsy teaches that immortality is within reach of the man devoted to a single high ideal. So with the institution: a group of men from Yale have tried to show that by unflinching faith a practical work may be accomplished and a new vitality earned. If conviction remains unshaken, support will come. The College which goes by the name of Ya-li in China represents their ideal; it is no more and no less a missionary College than Yale in New Haven, but so far as its supporters are concerned it is an effort of pure altruism. Both alike try to train students in accordance with Christian conceptions of personal honor and righteousness. To transplant some of the generative forces that inhere in a democratic institution like Yale a society was formed by graduates in 1902 which might emphasize sound scholarship in China and show how inevitably character is involved in training youth to real usefulness. As was proper in an enterprise of this sort, no responsibility or share in the scheme was assumed by the University as an organization, and care was taken not to interfere with collections elsewhere solicited for foreign missions. After a preliminary survey, Changsha, the capital of Hunan Province, was selected, with the approval of Christian missionaries located there, as a suitable center for locating a school which might in time influence the educational development of interior China.

This contribution of Yale to the welfare of a friendly nation, with no desire to subject her to an imported American control of education or her students to religious tests, was an entirely original idea. The result already attained is notable in every way. The Chinese, after a period of cautious observation, have crowded the class rooms to the number of two hundred; they have agreed to coöperate in building a Medical School and subscribed $25,000 annually for its support; they have asked and accepted the advice of Yale men in the management of their Red Cross Hospital, public hygiene, and the betterment of social conditions. Such cordial and intimate union between native and foreigner, voluntarily associated, is unknown elsewhere in China. The alumni of Yale have responded with increasing generosity to support the Society, contributing an annual budget now amounting to nearly $27,000, and about $250,000 for land and buildings, $150,000 of which is a single gift for a hospital now in course of erection; they have also supplied twenty-six graduates of various degrees to the faculties, two of whom have died in service. Buildings of a substantial type have been put on a campus of twenty acres outside of the city, where the School and College are housed close to the Medical School which purposes to train physicians and nurses as thoroughly as can be done anywhere in Asia. The China Medical Board of the Rockefeller Foundation after a critical examination has bestowed upon the latter the stamp of its expert approval and a subvention for the support of six teaching physicians with a promise of further assistance in furthering research work in medicine. Other American Colleges have taken up the challenge to altruism and made their contributions in different ways to improve conditions in the East. Considering the novelty of the undertaking and the wide interests involved, the achievement of Yale in China during ten years ranks among her noblest contributions to the welfare of the world.

GENERAL ALUMNI GIFTS TO YALE

By

SAMUEL R. BETTS

The gifts to Yale by her alumni and friends, if stated in any detail, would form a most interesting history, from that first gift of books by the Founders, and the benefactions of Elihu Yale and Bishop Berkeley, down to the subscription for equipment of the present Yale Battery. But the scope of this article is limited to gifts to the Corporation for which the entire body of Alumni have been invited to subscribe, and resulting in the establishment of permanent funds whose income is substantially unrestricted, or in buildings for University use. It includes also gifts which may be spent immediately as income, but are not designated for specific purposes. The Alumni funds or gifts of this character are five in number, and will be considered in chronological order.

First, the "CENTUM MILLIA FUND," so called because of the provision that "No subscription shall be obligatory, unless the sum of at least One Hundred Thousand Dollars shall be subscribed, before the first day of December, A. D. 1832." Each subscriber could designate the object to which his subscription should be applied, but otherwise payments were to be held as a permanent fund, of which the income only should be appropriated to the support of the Academical Department. The Yale Treasurer's Report refers to this as an invested fund of $82,950,

Established in 1832 from subscriptions received in the first movement for raising a large amount for general endowment. Of the $100,000.00 subscribed the above amount was given on condition that the Corporation should hold the amount and use the income only for the general purposes of Yale College. The balance has been distributed among the various departments for which it was subscribed.

Subscriptions ranged from one of $4, up to three of $5,000 each. The total subscription aggregated $105,938 from 606 individuals, many of them not graduates of Yale.

Second, the so-called "FUND OF 1854," listed in the Treasurer's Report at $69,601.10, and there described as

Established November 7th, 1854, by subscriptions to the second general movement for raising money for endowment. The amount subscribed was $106,390.92 and the difference between the amount shown above and this sum was distributed to the departments or objects specified by the donors. Income used for general purposes.

The appeal for this fund appears in a printed pamphlet dated New Haven, January 25, 1853, and is signed by Theodore D. Woolsey and Jeremiah Day, for the Corporation, and Benjamin Silliman, Chauncey A. Goodrich, and Denison Olmsted, for the Faculty. It was also specially endorsed by an influential New York committee, including Daniel Lord, 1814, William Adams, 1827, and William M. Evarts, 1837, and by resolution at the Yale Alumni meeting at Commencement, July, 1853. It is interesting to note that the leading basis of this appeal was the inadequate salaries of the instructors in the College, and that a contribution of $150,000 to the permanent funds of the College was asked. It was stated that the price of tuition, then $39 per annum, would necessarily be raised unless the desired fund was established. The following paragraph from this pamphlet is especially significant:

The increase of the price of tuition to anything near its cost, would drive from the College a very desirable class of students—those whose means are limited, but whose industrious habits and sound morals exert the most healthful influence. The College would become a college for the sons of the rich, to the exclusion of the sons of the middling classes, who have always been the reliance of the Institution, from their steadiness of character, their diligence in study, and their moral and religious worth. A College supported by the sons of the rich, it has been well remarked, will very soon become a place where the rich will not dare to send their sons.

The Treasurer's figures show that the full amount hoped for was not secured, in spite of the eloquent appeal and influential signers.

Third, the "WOOLSEY MEMORIAL FUND." This is a University fund, as distinguished from the two previously mentioned Yale College funds. It is listed at $172,451.97 in the Treasurer's Report, and described as

Established August 1st, 1873, by gifts from Alumni and Friends of the College under a resolution adopted at the meeting of the Alumni, in New Haven, July 13th, 1871, as a memorial of the work of Theodore Dwight Woolsey, Yale College 1820, President from 1846 to 1871. Income used for general purposes.

Committees of graduates representing different classes and different sections of the country were constituted, with permanent treasurer and secretary, and a thorough canvass was made of all graduates, including others who were friends of Yale. The amount obtained was not as large as hoped for, but after a canvass lasting two years, the subscription was closed and the fund established. This was the first University fund resulting from general Alumni subscription, and it anticipated by nearly fourteen years the legal designation of "Yale University."

Fourth, "THE BICENTENNIAL FUND." Although the Treasurer's Report does not show any invested fund under this name, it is considered proper to refer to the large subscriptions from Alumni and friends of the University made in connection with the Bicentennial Celebration in 1901, and amounting to $1,102,859.23. This sum was applied toward the cost of the so-called Bicentennial Buildings, including Woolsey Hall, Memorial Hall, and University Dining Hall. These Bicentennial funds were secured by appeals to all who had ever been connected with the University in any department, as well as to friends of the University. A representative finance committee was appointed, together with special committees and agents in different localities, departments, and classes.

Fifth, the "YALE ALUMNI UNIVERSITY FUND." In June, 1890, the Corporation established the "Alumni University Fund" in response to resolutions of the New York alumni, and at Commencement of that year there was organized an association "to be known as 'The Alumni University Fund Association,' to be managed by nine Directors, alumni of Yale, appointed by the President of the University." Everyone who has been a student in any School of the University is invited to join the Association by contributing to the Fund, and any contribution is sufficient qualification for membership. The fundamental object of the Association is to induce universal annual giving, and to encourage gifts of any size, however small, for general University use.

In the work of the Alumni Fund Association each graduating class is now represented by a Class Agent, appointed by the Directors of the Fund. Gifts may be either unrestricted or for addition to the Principal Fund. The Directors may award the entire unrestricted amount to be used as University Income, and may suggest the application thereof. For the last five years, at their request, it has been applied to increased salaries for the teaching force. Legacies, of which a number have been received, are added to the Principal Fund, as memorials to the donors. The Alumni Fund differs from all other funds of the University. It is controlled by Directors chosen from the graduates instead of by the University authorities alone, it increases every year, and it is unrestricted. Its principal is a part of the University endowment. The gifts from income of the Fund to University income are not confined to specific purposes.

For the first year of its existence, ending June, 1891, the Association reported 385 members and total "cash received into the Fund, $11,015.08." Compare with this the report for the year ending June 30, 1916, showing more than 4,000 contributors, and total gross receipts of $146,280.53 of which $70,000.00 was appropriated as income, and $72,746.63 was added to principal fund.

The receipts from the inauguration of the Fund, in 1890, to June 30, 1916, reached the grand total of $1,600,222.63, of which $870,213.57 remains as principal fund, and $702,137.89, has been given the University for annual income, the total expenses of management being only $27,871.17.

With the experience of the past twenty-five years as a guide, and the success already attained, and the constant introduction of more efficient methods of interesting Yale men, there is confidence on the part of those who have inaugurated and carried forward this Alumni Fund that far greater results will be obtained in the future.

OFFICERS OF THE PAGEANT

AND

MEMBERS OF COMMITTEES

AND

ORGANIZATIONS PARTICIPATING

IN THE PAGEANT

PAGEANT EXECUTIVE

Master of the Pageant
FRANCIS HARTMAN MARKOE

Master of the Music DAVID STANLEY SMITH	*Editor of the Book* GEORGE HENRY NETTLETON
Artist of the Pageant MISS CHRISTINE HERTER	*Mistress of the Robes* MRS. DENNIS CLEUGH
Stage Manager DENNIS CLEUGH	*Assistant Director* JACK RANDALL CRAWFORD
Business Manager FREDERIC BLAIR JOHNSON	*Director of Publicity* CHARLES EMERSON COOK

GENERAL COMMITTEE

MR. ELI WHITNEY, *Chairman*
MR. EDWIN ROGERS EMBREE, *Secretary*

REVEREND JOSEPH ANDERSON
MR. OTTO TREMONT BANNARD
PROFESSOR HIRAM BINGHAM
PROFESSOR BERTRAM BORDEN BOLTWOOD
DIRECTOR RUSSELL HENRY CHITTENDEN
DEAN WILBUR LUCIUS CROSS
MR. JOSEPH BENJAMIN DIMMICK
MR. LOOMIS HAVEMEYER
DEAN FREDERICK SHEETZ JONES
DIRECTOR WILLIAM SERGEANT KENDALL
MR. VANCE CRISWELL MCCORMICK
MR. BURTON MANSFIELD
MR. FRANCIS HARTMAN MARKOE
PROFESSOR CLARENCE WHITTLESEY MENDELL
MR. PAYSON MERRILL
DEAN HORATIO WILLIAM PARKER
PROFESSOR WILLIAM LYON PHELPS
MR. GEORGE DUDLEY SEYMOUR
PROFESSOR DAVID STANLEY SMITH
REVEREND ANSON PHELPS STOKES

EXECUTIVE COMMITTEE

MR. FRANCIS HARTMAN MARKOE, *Chairman*
MR. EDWIN ROGERS EMBREE, *Secretary*
MR. HOWELL CHENEY   MR. FREDERIC BLAIR JOHNSON
PROFESSOR CLARENCE WHITTLESEY MENDELL

The Executive Committee which made the early plans for the celebration of the two hundredth anniversary of the removal of Yale College to New Haven was composed of Reverend Anson Phelps Stokes, *Chairman;* the late Professor John Christopher Schwab, *Secretary;* and Mr. Eli Whitney.

FINANCE COMMITTEE

Mr. Eli Whitney, *Chairman*

Mr. Howell Cheney Mr. Henry Bradford Sargent

COMMITTEE ON AUTHORS

Dean Wilbur Lucius Cross, *Chairman*

Professor John Milton Berdan Professor George Henry Nettleton

Professor William Lyon Phelps

COMMITTEE ON GRADUATE PARTICIPATION

Mr. Joseph Benjamin Dimmick, *Chairman*

Mr. Frank Lewis Bigelow Mr. William Scranton Pardee

Mr. Henry Stuart Hotchkiss Mr. Edward Johnson Phelps

Mr. Burton Mansfield Mr. Lucius Franklin Robinson

COMMITTEE ON UNDERGRADUATE PARTICIPATION

Professor Edward Bliss Reed, *Chairman*

Professor Hollon Augustine Farr Mr. Herbert Harold Vreeland, Jr.

CITIZENS COMMITTEE

Mayor Frank James Rice, *Chairman*

Mr. Frederick Dibble Adams Mr. Charles Edward Julin

Mr. Ellis Benjamin Baker Mr. John Baldwin Kennedy

Dr. Charles Joseph Bartlett Mr. Eli Mix

Mr. Winchester Bennett Rabbi Louis Leopold Mann

Mr. Dennis Albert Blakeslee Reverend Oscar Edward Maurer

Mr. Walter Camp Mr. James Thomas Moran

Mr. Samuel Campner Mr. William John George Myers

Mr. Livingston Warner Cleaveland Mr. Norris Galpin Osborn

Mr. William Perry Curtiss Mr. Sylvester Zesserino Poli

Mr. John Dalgleish Mr. John Keeler Punderford

Mr. Frederick Luther Ford Mr. Edward Payson Root

Mr. Frederick David Grave Mr. Rudolph Steinert

Reverend Andrew Francis Harty Mr. Louis Ezekiel Stoddard

Mr. George Marshall Hayes Mr. Nathan Beach Stone

Mr. William Austin Hendrick Mr. Philip Troup

Mr. Joseph Edward Hubinger Mr. Isaac Morris Ullman

Mr. John Day Jackson Mr. Charles Morehead Walker

Mr. Joseph Charles Johnson Mr. Stephen Whitney

Mr. Kenneth Wynne

CITIZENS EXECUTIVE COMMITTEE

Mayor Frank James Rice, *Chairman*

Mr. Samuel Campner Mr. James Thomas Moran

Mr. Joseph Edward Hubinger Mr. Louis Ezekiel Stoddard

Mr. Isaac Morris Ullman

ORGANIZATIONS PARTICIPATING
IN THE PAGEANT

FANFARE

Undertaken by—THE CLASS OF 1919 AND THE ORCHESTRA.

PRELUDE

Undertaken by—THE SCHOOL OF MEDICINE; THE COLLEGE CHOIR AND GLEE CLUB; SAINT MARY'S CHURCH; THE UNITED CHURCH; THE COLONIAL DAMES; MRS. EDWARD B. REED, MR. H. H. VREELAND, JR.

Episode Secretaries—MRS. H. SAXTON BURR, MRS. EDWARD B. REED, MRS. WILLISTON WALKER, THE REVEREND FATHER CYPRIAN MARCHANT, MR. H. W. HAGGARD, MR. H. H. VREELAND, JR.

FIRST EPISODE

Undertaken by—THE CLASS OF 1917 S.; THE SCHOOL OF FORESTRY; FIRST CHURCH OF CHRIST; DAVENPORT CHURCH; PILGRIM CHURCH; TAYLOR CHURCH; TRINITY CHURCH; IMPROVED ORDER OF RED MEN—HAMMONASSETT TRIBE NO. 1, AND NINIGRET TRIBE NO. 55; DEGREE OF POCAHONTAS—NARKEETA COUNCIL NO. 27; ST. PAUL'S GIRLS' FRIENDSHIP LEAGUE; MISS RUTH R. LEVINE.

Episode Secretaries—MISS RUTH R. LEVINE, MISS M. ELIZABETH WELCH, MRS. F. H. WIGGIN, THE REVEREND OSCAR E. MAURER, MR. C. E. BEHRE, MR. ST.C. T. CORSON, MR. R. P. NEWTON, MR. JOHN P. STREET, MR. J. H. WARE, JR., MR. NOAH A. WEINER.

Episode Mistresses of Robes—MRS. HOWARD W. BEACH, MISS FLORENCE BROWN, MRS. JOHN P. STREET, MRS. I. BODINE VALLÉ.

Episode Master of Robes—MR. THOMAS KELLEY.

FIRST INTERLUDE

Undertaken by—THE ASSOCIATION OF COLLEGIATE ALUMNAE AND THE SCHOOL CHILDREN OF NEW HAVEN.

Episode Secretaries—MRS. EDWARD UHL AND MR. H. J. SCHNELLE.

Episode Mistresses of Robes—MRS. A. W. LEIGHTON AND MISS J. R. MESSER.

SECOND EPISODE.

Undertaken by—THE CLASS OF 1917; SECOND COMPANY OF THE GOVERNOR'S FOOT GUARD; COMPANY F, 2D. INFANTRY, C. N. G. ("NEW HAVEN GRAYS"); TROOP A CAVALRY, C. N. G.; THE SONS OF VETERANS; THE DAUGHTERS OF THE AMERICAN REVOLUTION—EVE LEAR CHAPTER, MARY CLAP WOOSTER CHAPTER, SUSAN CARRINGTON CLARKE CHAPTER (MERIDEN), MILLICENT PORTER CHAPTER (WATERBURY), RUTH HART CHAPTER (MERIDEN), ELIZABETH CLARKE HULL CHAPTER (ANSONIA), SARAH RIGGS HUMPHREYS CHAPTER (DERBY), SARAH LUDLOW CHAPTER (SEYMOUR); THE YOUNG WOMEN'S CHRISTIAN ASSOCIATION; NEW HAVEN CALEDONIAN CLUB.

Episode Secretaries—MISS INEZ HULL, MRS. FREDERICK W. PECK, MRS. HUBERT M. SEDGWICK, MAJOR J. B. KENNEDY, CAPTAIN ELLIS B. BAKER, JR., CAPTAIN F. E. WOLF, MR. O. B. CUNNINGHAM, MR. ELLERY S. JAMES, MR. ROBERT MACARTHUR, SR., MR. GEORGE DUDLEY SEYMOUR.

Episode Mistresses of Robes—MRS. F. W. HODGE, MRS. INEZ H. KNOWLTON, MRS. JAMES L. NESBIT.

Episode Master of Robes—MR. R. P. PFLIEGER.

SECOND INTERLUDE

Undertaken by—THE NAVAL MILITIA; UNITED SPANISH WAR VETERANS—ALLAN M. OSBORN CAMP NO. 1; CATHOLIC LADIES SOCIETY; TEMPLE MISHKAN ISRAEL; ST. AGNES TEMPERANCE SOCIETY; EQUAL FRANCHISE LEAGUE; THE NEW HAVEN WOMAN'S CLUB; INTERNATIONAL SUNSHINE SOCIETY—CYNTHIA WESTOVER ALDEN BRANCH, FORT WOOSTER BRANCH, CANONICUS BRANCH (NEW BRITAIN), MARY PARRISH BRANCH (WATERBURY); UNIVERSAL SUNSHINE SOCIETY—ELM CITY BRANCH, COREOPSIS BRANCH, MAYFLOWER BRANCH; THE CAMP FIRE GIRLS; P. O. U. SOCIAL CLUB; THE TEACHERS OF NEW HAVEN; BOYS FROM THE GRAMMAR AND HIGH SCHOOLS OF NEW HAVEN; SCHOOL CHILDREN OF NEW HAVEN; UNITED WORKERS BOYS' CLUB; A GROUP OF UNATTACHED PERFORMERS; MRS. EDWARD G. BUCKLAND, MISS E. MARJORIE STALEY.

Episode Secretaries—MRS. R. F. ARMSTRONG, MRS. JOHN J. CARROLL, MRS. G. LEROY CLARK, MISS M. G. CLARK, MRS. J. E. COBEY, MISS HELEN L. GILBERT, MRS. LOUIS C. HELLER, MRS. D. C. SAUNDERS, MISS WINIFRED SMYTH, MRS. J. W. TABB, MRS. JOSEPHA WHITNEY, LIEUTENANT COMMANDER CLIFFORD M. PECK, MR. R. L. LOVELL, MR. H. J. SCHNELLE, MR. WALTER K. QUIGLEY.

Episode Mistresses of Robes—MISS ESTHER CARR, MRS. HARRY C. EDWARDS, MRS. JOSEPH GALLOND, MRS. FLORA W. LOCKWOOD, MISS J. R. MESSER, MRS. HENRY L. PARDEE, MRS. F. HOWARD RUSSELL, MISS WINIFRED SMYTH, MRS. ISADORE WERZBERG.

THIRD EPISODE

Undertaken by—THE CLASSES OF 1918, 1919, AND 1918 S.; THE GRADUATE SCHOOL; THE SCHOOL OF THE FINE ARTS; THE SCHOOL OF LAW; THE YALE SOUTHERN CLUB; COMPANY I, 7TH. REGIMENT, N. Y.; DEPARTMENT OF CONNECTICUT G. A. R.; NEW HAVEN POLICE DEPARTMENT; NEW HAVEN FIRE DEPARTMENT; SAVIN ROCK HOSE COMPANY NO. 4; THE GRAND AVENUE CHURCH; THE CHURCH OF THE REDEEMER; MISS JOSEPHINE FOSTER, MISS L. WATERS.

Episode Secretaries—MRS. WALTER F. BISHOP, MISS MARGARET S. CARHART, MISS GERTRUDE LINNELL, CAPTAIN WADE H. HAYES, DR. B. A. CHENEY, THE REVEREND BOYLE HOUGHTON, CHIEF PHILIP T. SMITH, CHIEF RUFUS R. FANCHER, MR. E. H. CLARK, JR., MR. T. N. CRAWFORD, MR. W. E. DONALDSON, MR. CHARLES W. ESTILL, MR. A. V. HEELY, MR. M. S. KIMBALL, MR. A. SIDNEY LYNCH, MR. G. M. MCBRIDE, MR. R. J. MENNER, MR. B. R. MYLES, MR. F. J. WALLS.

Episode Mistresses of Robes—MRS. WALLACE HURLBURT AND MRS. R. P. TYLER.

THIRD INTERLUDE

Undertaken by—MRS. JACK RANDALL CRAWFORD AND MISS REBECCA D. GIBBONS.

FOURTH EPISODE

Undertaken by—THE STUDENTS OF ALL CLASSES; THE NEW HAVEN ALUMNI ASSOCIATION; AND THE YALE BATTERY.

Episode Secretaries—CLASS SECRETARIES, COLONEL ROBERT MELVILLE DANFORD, AND MR. E. B. UNDERWOOD.

FINALE

Undertaken by—THE WIVES OF THE OFFICERS OF YALE UNIVERSITY; AND MRS. J. MARSHALL FLINT AND MRS. HENRY H. TOWNSHEND.

THE TUTTLE, MOREHOUSE & TAYLOR COMPANY